This book belongs to:

_____

The Fight For Focus

Embracing

Adult ADHD

An Insightful Guide to Help Adults
Understand and Strengthen
Executive Functioning

"I am honored to help you on **your journey.** Begin owning your neurodiversity!"

-Melinda Riley

ISBN-13: 979-8768166281 (Hardcover)
ISBN-13: 979-8767942831 (Paperback)

www.melindarileybooks.com

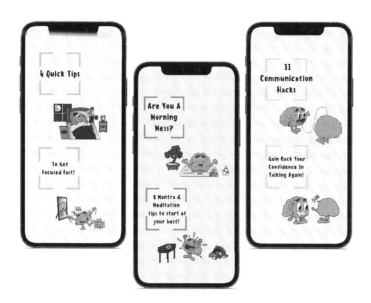

A Special Gift To Our Readers

Included with your purchase of this book is our Winning with ADHD 3-series Bundle! This series will aid you with quick tools that can be applied to your everyday life. This gift was created to make you smile and laugh with funny relatable brain comics which I sincerely hope you enjoy!

To receive your special gift, click the link below or scan the QR code and follow the directions on the page.

- Much Love, Melinda Riley

**https://winwithadhd.activeho
sted.com/f/1**

TABLE OF
CONTENTS

INTRODUCTION

Have you ever started a task, and found yourself in the midst of fifty other projects before realizing that the initial task has been left half-finished? I certainly have. That's part of executive dysfunction, and it's not something that you should blame yourself for. To a certain degree, everyone gets distracted, but from a neurological perspective, ADHD physically takes this inability to settle one's mind on a specific task to a whole new level. I've struggled with executive dysfunction myself, but when my sister, Renesmee, was diagnosed with ADHD, I gained a newfound appreciation for the meaning of the diagnosis and dedicated myself to learning how to help. Renesmee struggles with focus *a lot*. She'll sit down to work on something on her laptop, do 20 minutes of work, suddenly become aware that she's hungry, and be halfway through making paninis for the entire family before remembering what she was supposed to be working on. She has missed deadlines because she has genuinely just forgotten that they existed, and she has lost friends because she's an "out of sight out of mind" kind of person and that doesn't gel with the neurotypical need for consistency in relationships.

Having ADHD isn't always easy, and my sister—like so many neurodivergent people—hasn't always been kind to herself about the various symptoms involved. For a long time, Renesmee saw her inability to complete tasks as a character flaw. She felt that if she tried harder, or cared more, this wouldn't have to be such an issue. That was the mindset that one teacher after another had drilled into her head over years of formal education. Every school report came home with several comments along the lines of, "Good student, but needs to try harder," or "Needs to apply herself more, exam results disappointing."

Like any young and impressionable girl, Renesmee internalized these remarks not just as a reflection of her academics, but of who she was.

Over the years, my sister has tried every kind of organizational technique in the book. She tried apps that reward you for not getting distracted by your phone, ones that make a little plant grow for every task you complete or feed a bunny for each hour you spend focused. She's tried post-it notes on the bathroom mirror, journaling, tricking her brain into thinking that deadlines are earlier than they really are, reward systems, punishment systems, the carrot, and the stick. All that this led to was a sense of shame and self-blame that she just couldn't shake. The only thing that has truly made a difference to her mental and emotional well-being, as well as her ability to manage her ADHD, has been to come to terms with her neurodivergence and learn to work with it, rather than against it.

That is what drove me to write this book. There is far too much stigma surrounding ADHD. People think of it as the "Ooh, look! A squirrel!" disorder that can only present itself in hyper little boys, and that common misconception only heightens the isolation felt by many people when they are trying to learn how to manage the condition. I adore my sister and supporting her through her diagnosis and learning how to cope with it has been an eye-opening experience. In our large Caribbean family, celebrations of life flow in our veins, so to see Renesmee struggling to accept herself for who she was only made me all the more determined to learn everything I possibly could about neurodiversity. She deserved a better quality of life—which, thankfully, we have been able to build together—and so do you.

For too long, executive dysfunction has been presented and seen as "laziness" or "procrastination," and far too few neurotypicals seem to

2

understand that with executive dysfunction, you can *want* to do the task, know *how* to do the task, and most likely even have the *energy* to do the task, but your brain simply won't allow you to actually get up and do it. That isn't a reflection of who you are as a person; it's a sign that you need to learn how to manage your time and energy around the needs of your neurological differences, and that's okay!

No one—but in particular not anyone who is neurodivergent—should feel that they are in any way broken and trying to cope using techniques designed by and for neurotypical people only exacerbates this sense that they will never fit in or find success. Allow me to reassure you, that is not the point of this book. While I will be offering some guidance, all of the information and skills included in this book are backed by science and the testimonials of neurodiverse people themselves. This won't be a quick-fix tutorial on how to mask your symptoms to fit in with a neurotypical world, or a rule book of how to function "appropriately" in a capitalistic society that values productivity over mental and physical health. Instead, this book is about giving you the tools to create your own sense of mastery over your life. It's about granting you the freedom and mental clarity to embrace your neurodivergence rather than feel ashamed of it, and it's about building the support systems and internal confidence to get you through the ebbs and flows that are a natural part of the way your brain works.

I am on a mission to educate the neurotypicals of the world that different does not mean inadequate, but more importantly, I want to help people with executive dysfunction learn to embrace what control they do have in their lives, to release the fear and anxiety that surround what they can't control, and to find their voice and their freedom. Understanding and respecting our differences is key to the physical and mental health of the neurodiverse. After all, masking of symptoms has repeatedly been negatively correlated with well-being. I have seen the ways that my friends and family members have been able to drastically improve their quality of life by accommodating their needs and respecting their limits instead of seeing them as flaws, and I want to help others who struggle with executive functioning to do the same. I respect that the people who live with any condition are the experts in that condition, and do not intend to speak over the neurodivergent community—nothing about you without you. My role here is simply to pass on the information that I have discovered through my years of research which I have seen truly help my neurodivergent loved ones.

Over the course of my years of research since my sister received her diagnosis, I have watched her grow from the shy, self-conscious, self-critical girl she once was and blossom into the woman that she is today—a fully realized version of herself who understands and embodies her differences with confidence. I have witnessed firsthand how empowering it was for her to figure out and accept why her brain worked differently from the socially accepted "norm", and to learn that she didn't need to fight to fit in with the rigidity of neurotypical ideals. Renesmee hasn't actually changed anything about herself throughout all my research and our various little experiments with coping mechanisms. She hasn't needed to, because that's not what any of this is about. If anything, my sister is now far more comfortable with being and expressing her true self than she once was; plagued as she was by the idea of being the "weird girl" if she stepped a toe outside the neurotypical norm. This is the kind of freedom that I want to share with others through this book.

Throughout this book's chapters, I will guide you through recognizing the reach of the ways in which ADHD impacts your life, and understanding that your neurodivergence can be your *strength*, not your weakness. We will take a look at some common myths surrounding ADHD, and challenge the ridiculous notions that often surround the condition in common parlance. We'll contemplate how to go about accepting the differences in the ways your brain works, and how crucial it is to hold compassion for yourself as you come to terms with these differences. And, most importantly, I will guide you through creating an environment in which you feel supported and respected, both internally in your mind, and externally, by respectfully asserting your needs and boundaries with the people around you. By preparing for the times when your executive dysfunction flares with particular severity, and creating a safety net of coping mechanisms to fall back on during these inevitable struggles, you can grant yourself permission to give your mind and body the rest that they so desperately crave without being at risk of slipping into old patterns of self-condemnation. I will also include a few random fun facts at various intervals, as I know how difficult it can be to focus on non-fiction, even when we're aware that it would be beneficial to us to do so. I hope that these "Brain Breaks" will ease your progress through this book and provide a helpful experience overall.

You deserve to feel proud of yourself. You deserve to take life at your own pace without being made to feel shame for operating differently. You don't have to feel trapped in a cycle of overachievement and burnout. You don't have to feel that executive dysfunction translates to laziness, be paralyzed by that kind of thinking, or buy into the idea that your self-worth is inherently linked to your productivity. You have intrinsic worth as a human being. Everyone's brain learns, remembers, and manages tasks differently, and you don't see neurotypical people beating themselves up for needing to do practical tasks themselves to understand them, so neither should you be feeling ashamed of having to ask people to repeat themselves because of auditory processing delays. Everyone's abilities fluctuate from day to day based on factors like their mood, how much sleep they got, if they're hungry, and so on. The fact that your fluctuations are more pronounced is not a flaw. The very idea that it could be a flaw is a reflection of society's inability to tolerate difference, not a reflection on your character or value as a person.

There are ways to manage your symptoms and build a life you feel comfortable with, without having to reject your neurodivergence. Navigating a world not built for you is an exhausting experience, particularly when you don't have the right tools to help you on that path, but with a little education and a few adjustments in perspective, those coping mechanisms are there to be grasped. With these skills, what you once thought of as "laziness" can become restful rejuvenation, free from the guilt that so often comes from misinterpreting executive dysfunction. Your overthinking can become the means to coping with potential problems ahead of time and being able to release those anxieties. Your task jumping that can be mislabeled "chaotic" can become the evolutionary advantage that makes you the master multitasker. Essentially, you can feel competent, in control, and have compassion for yourself.

I won't recommend that you plaster your neurodivergence in toxic positivity, or expect you to conform to neurotypical ideals. These kinds of quick fixes never work, and only ever lead to more disordered thinking and inner criticism. Besides which, you aren't broken, so you don't need to be "fixed." Instead, I ask you to join me on the journey that I once took with my beloved sister, and have since taken with many neurodivergent friends and family members. Whether you were diagnosed as a child, as an adult, or are just now in the process of considering seeking an official diagnosis, together we can work towards your version of personal empowerment and fulfillment. Together we can discover the true roots of the fight for focus, and together we can grant you the mental and emotional freedom to own your neurodiversity.

CHAPTER 1
Executive (Dys)Function — What and Why?

Every time that you remember something for a moment as you grab a pen to write it down, every instance where you tune out someone's loud chewing, every occasion that you bite your tongue when you're dealing with strong emotions, or notice that you are beginning to get overwhelmed, those are all examples of putting your executive functioning into action. Executive functioning is essentially the driver of your day-to-day tasks. It's the segment of your cognitive skills that allows you to access your working memory to use old information in new situations. It enables you to ignore irrelevant stimuli from the outside world and take in the task at hand. Executive functioning is even the part of your mind that gives you that opportunity to notice your emotional reaction to a situation and take a second to decide how to act. Any circumstance in which you need to follow ordered steps, reach a goal, or make a decision involves this type of cognition.

Some people have by-the-book mental drivers; their executive functioning follows the rules of the road, allows them to plan and follow through on focused tasks, stay organized, and keep track of a variety of scheduled responsibilities and obligations. Others go on autopilot sometimes. We put our brains on cruise control and so long as we get to the destination, things like mirror-signal-mirror-maneuver only come out on our driving test. But metaphors aside, most—if not all—cognitive functions are a spectrum. Everyone has their strengths. But though it can certainly present challenges sometimes, being less adept with one skill set or another is not necessarily a weakness.

Executive functioning itself can be broken into further subcategories, and each of these has its own potential to help or hinder our overall abilities based on individual strengths and the ways in which they are applied. **Attentional control is the aspect of cognition that allows us to selectively dedicate our attention to a given situation, task, or person**. It is the part of executive functioning that allows you to hear your name being spoken in a crowded room, or zone in on the face of the person you know in a busy street. It's the aspect that allows us to take in relevant information when and as we need it.

Cognitive flexibility, on the other hand, **is the facet of executive functioning that allows you to manage more than one thought pattern or emotional response at a time.** This is the mental capacity that gives us the ability to "go with the flow" and swap between tasks as needed. The degree to which we can use this flexibility varies over our lifespan. Researchers have noted since the mid-1960s that our neural pathways become more and more entrenched in their patterns as we age. Our brains are essentially muscles, and like any other muscle, its strength comes from the way that we use it. Put simply, the more often we think a certain type of thought, the stronger we become at thinking in that way again. Children have the benefit of encountering new experiences, and therefore thinking new types of thoughts, very often. This is not the case for adults, and we settle into a neurological routine that diminishes cognitive flexibility. Serotonin also plays a large part in the area of the brain responsible for shifting focus—the Anterior Cingulate Cortex—and therefore, conditions that impact serotonin levels, such as depression or PTSD, can cause changes to cognitive flexibility. These changes, in turn, impact one's ability to regulate their emotions and create part of the presentation of symptoms we associate with these kinds of conditions.

Tied into these concepts of cognitive flexibility and attentional control, is another form of executive functioning: cognitive inhibition. **Cognitive inhibition is the element that allows us to ignore irrelevant information.** Just as attentional control allows us to zone in on important stimuli, cognitive inhibition is the flipside of the coin that enables us to tune out what's unimportant. It endows us with the ability to choose what to ignore, to a certain degree. Of course, anyone's brain would be addled by a car alarm or a crying baby. For many people, neurodivergent and neurotypical alike, even a ticking clock or flickering lightbulb can be difficult to shut out. I personally can never ignore the incredibly loud flush of an airplane toilet; it just grates on me no matter what seat I'm in on the plane. But, cognitive inhibition does enable us to ignore an itchy insect bite, to drive while kids are chatting in the back seat, and to mentally step away from overwhelming emotions when we need to continue on as normal, such as when a vital presentation at work needs to be made shortly after a heated disagreement with a colleague.

We aren't born with this capability; cognitive inhibition is generally an adaptation that occurs when we are about three or four years old. As adults, reflecting on our earliest memories, we will often find that they come from roughly around this age. That is because this was the age when we were learning to take in only the information that was relevant to our situation, and thus detailed memories were able to be formed without overwhelming our senses. Before you knew how to tune out irrelevant sensory input, your brain was processing too much at once to possibly remember it all. This cognitive ability continues to develop as we age, and thus our memories become more and more specific to our personal circumstances. Cognitive inhibition also plays a role in the development of dissociative disorders in the cases of extreme childhood trauma. As noted in the 2004 *Handbook of Evolutionary Psychology*, "In situations involving treacherous acts by a caregiver, a 'cognitive information blockage' may occur that results in an isolation of knowledge of the event from awareness". This explains the often disputed phenomenon of repressed memories. When children are forced to remain dependent on the people that have hurt them, they will simply block out the knowledge of the abuse as a method of coping. This is an example of cognitive inhibition in overdrive.

<u>Inhibitory control</u> refers to the capacity to withhold one's own impulses rather than their thoughts or memories. This has been studied, for example, by assessing a child's ability to refrain from peeking at a present or to stifle their expression of disappointment at receiving an unsatisfying gift (Carlson & Wang, 2007). As we age, inhibitory control becomes a key factor in our ability to consider the impacts of our behavior on both ourselves and other people. Unfortunately, an overdevelopment of this skill can lead to the type of people-pleasing behavior that results in a complete suppression of one's true self. Leading trauma expert Dr. Bessel van der Kolk has shown that, in the long term, this self-betrayal can cause similar impacts to the brain as would a stroke or physical lesion, as witnessed through fMRI scans. Yet, more appropriate use of inhibitory control allows us to empathize with and include others. It also allows us to recognize when short-term discomfort is necessary for long-term success. We see the growth of this cognitive skill set in children who are able to prevent themselves from acting out in the hopes of impressing Santa. Their ability to recognize and implement delayed gratification is thanks to their developing executive functioning.

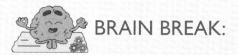

BRAIN BREAK:

When frogs eat, they use their eyeballs to swallow! ("All About Frogs", 2021)

Frogs ingest their prey whole, and their eyeballs are used in swallowing by sinking into their mouth to push the food down into their throats. Personally, I'm fairly relieved that humans use our tongues for this process. I doubt so many first dates would occur at restaurants if eating involved sucking our eyeballs into our heads!

The final subcategory of executive functioning is working memory. **Working memory is the temporary storage facility of your brain.** It has been theorized that this section of our memory can only handle a limited number of "chunks" of information. In order to remember anything more, some parts of the data will need to be transferred into our short-term, and eventually long-term, memory storage. In psychological circles, this is referred to as Miller's Law, crediting George Miller's foundational discovery of the limitations in 1956.

Miller proposed that human working memory can generally handle seven "chunks" of information; plus or minus two, dependent on personal abilities. However, these chunks are of variable sizes. This is why it's easier to remember a phone number by breaking it down into chunks of two to four numbers per section, rather than trying to remember each number individually.

Attentional control, cognitive flexibility, cognitive inhibition, inhibitory control, and working memory, combine to enable us to compile and analyze information, make and follow through on plans, regulate our emotions and thoughts, and see things from the perspective of others. We've briefly looked at what can occur in some instances where there is an overapplication of some of these abilities. But, what happens when they are impeded to some degree?

When executive functioning is impaired, it can sometimes lead to struggles in different areas of life, including school, work, and relationships. After all, even if you have all the motivation in the world, without the organizational skills to focus this drive, you're bound to have difficulty channeling that motivation. People who struggle with executive functioning will have trouble prioritizing and initiating tasks, choosing when to do them, and transitioning from one stage in a task to another. In adults, this can present itself as making minor mistakes with the details of complex tasks, struggling to focus in the workplace, difficulty remembering where they have left things, fidgeting, or difficulty waiting for one's turn in a conversation. Coincidentally, these are all also examples of criteria for an ADHD diagnosis under the Diagnostic and Statistical Manual of Medical Disorders, fifth edition (DSM-5).

When a large combination of executive functioning difficulties occur, this is referred to as executive dysfunction, or executive function deficit—a term that I personally loathe, since different regulation of a skill does not imply a "lack of function"—and has long been linked with ADHD and autism. Executive dysfunction does, however, occur in everyone to some degree. We all know someone who gets "hangry"—angry when they're hungry—and this is simply a case of hunger dysregulating their inhibitory control of their emotions. Likewise, other physical vulnerabilities such as tiredness or alcohol and substance use can also affect our ability to focus our attention, regulate our emotions, make decisions, etc.

There are many ways that such executive dysfunction can present itself to cause or contribute to other symptoms. For instance, declines in executive functioning are one of the earlier signs of the onset of dementia. Compromised working memory and attentional control have been linked with amnesia in schizophrenia patients (Oram, Geffen, Geffen, Kavanagh & McGrath, 2005). In individuals with bipolar disorder, inhibitory control struggles contribute to impulsive behavior whilst in manic phases (Robinson et al., 2006). Research published in the *European Journal of Neurology* showed that, in patients with Parkinson's Disease, impairments to spatial working memory exacerbated neuromotor symptoms. Thus, people with ADHD are far from the only people affected by the impacts of executive dysfunction.

Whatever the underlying cause or overriding diagnosis, issues with executive functioning can cause a lot of difficulty in keeping up with the "grind culture" associated with late-stage capitalism. When more and more people are being forced to take on second or even third jobs to keep up with the ever-increasing costs of living, struggling to organize one's time can feel like a huge disadvantage, and difficulty with sustained attention rules out a lot of administrative or repetitive forms of employment. But what we currently label as "dysfunction" has not always been seen in this way, and indeed still isn't seen this way in many non-Westernized societies. A 2008 study of nomadic tribes in northern Kenya showed that a decrease in executive functioning led to an increase in the successful obtaining of food, and thus, survival (Eisenberg et al., 2008). With less inhibition and potential to overthink, hunter-gatherers who would be labeled "dysfunctional" in office employment, were extremely successful at adapting to changing environments.

Likewise, up until relatively recently, children were taught important ethical lessons quite informally. Play and stories were used to encourage certain types of behavior and understanding, rather than the rigid classroom settings that we are used to in the modern era. In these less structured environments, what is now labeled as ADHD or autism was once labeled as a thirst for knowledge, since children were encouraged to ask off-topic questions and follow their own trains of thought. Now, a child is more likely to be told, "We're not covering that until next year," than to be praised for lateral thinking. Because of this, though I will be using the term "executive dysfunction" throughout this book, I encourage you to see this as a variation in neurological processing rather than a fault. Don't get caught up in the "dys-" prefix. This attribution of moral standards to scientific labels can unfortunately only add to the stigmatization of executive dysfunction that causes so many parents to choose not to "label" their child with a diagnosis when doing so would grant them access to the kind of supports they may desperately need.

Like the social model of disability states, the nature of what makes someone disabled isn't their condition or symptoms, but rather the structures and attitudes of society that act as an impediment to those who fall outside of the norm. The labeling of any "disorder" is only giving a title to a collection of departures from that norm. Yet, in terms of Attention Deficit Hyperactivity Disorder, this title seems a bit of a misnomer. I can't help but notice that this set of symptoms is entitled according to the ways in which they irritate intolerant neurotypicals, and not the underlying neurological processes or the effects on the individual experiencing them. Rather than a deficit of attention, people with ADHD instead struggle to regulate the focus of their attention. Hyperactivity could just as easily be labeled impulse dysregulation. As you will see in the following chapter, the base neurological differences in people with ADHD would lend credence to the argument that ADHD should instead be called 'Dopamine Depression', and I do not doubt that there would be significantly more sympathy for the condition if this were the case. But, regardless of the labels applied to symptoms and their groupings, it is vital that we learn to recognize the signs of executive dysfunction and understand their significance. If you have ever had the thought, "I just can't" about a given task, you were likely experiencing a certain amount of executive dysfunction. We need to be capable of recognizing and addressing when this form of cognition starts to impact our daily lives, and how to help ourselves when it does.

Executive dysfunction causes difficulty with both starting tasks and seeing them through to completion, and this inertia can be exacerbated by any further demands on our cognitive functions, such as stress. As mentioned in the introduction, this immobilization is *not* laziness or procrastination rather, but a neurophysiological incapacity. It doesn't matter how much you might want to do something; if executive dysfunction has its way, you will remain right where you are. Neurotypical society has a tendency to think that this only applies to either boring tasks like homework, or frivolous things like whether or not to get an ice cream out of the freezer. But executive dysfunction has the potential to impact every corner of your life, including vital self-care tasks such as feeding oneself, going to the bathroom, showering, etc. And while difficulty with these tasks is often seen as a symptom of depression, it is important that medical professionals remain cognizant that the "hyperactive" part of ADHD refers to impulse control, not necessarily physical movement or productivity.

Similarly, always being late is a common impact of executive dysfunction that is sometimes misattributed to social anxiety. People think that if you don't show up on time to an event, that's somehow an indication that you didn't want to be there in the first place, but in some cases, you just physically can't get out the door. Executive dysfunction commonly presents itself as problems with effective multitasking, trouble remembering and following instructions, and high levels of distractibility. However, it also shows up as time blindness—an inability to feel time passing or guesstimate what time it is—difficulty breaking large tasks down into manageable steps, and anxiety at a disruption to one's routine. It is a common ableist trope to label these issues as laziness, apathy, or ingratitude for opportunities. Yet, in reality, they can be important signs pointing to a deeper need for support. Executive dysfunction can be indicative of a variety of potential diagnoses, and it's important that medical professionals learn to differentiate between how this presents in people with neurological conditions or brain injuries, from those with childhood trauma, or those under the influence of stimuli such as high-sugar food or drugs. In each case, when and how executive dysfunction presents itself will be slightly different, and each will require its own perspective on treatment. Therefore, overarching stereotypes of what executive dysfunction means about you as a person are complete and utter garbage. They don't even point to one diagnosis, never mind a single personality type!

A recently completed study of several thousand people in the Netherlands linked delays in developing executive cognition during childhood. Thus contributing to a 40% increase in the likelihood of an eventual diagnosis of Autism Spectrum Disorder (ASD), and three times the likelihood of being diagnosed with ADHD (Otterman et al., 2019). So, wouldn't it be great if we could learn to recognize this difference in development and teach these kids from a very young age that their way of functioning is okay? If they were given the coping mechanisms that usually are only presented after an official diagnosis, would there ever be a need to label those children as "disordered" at all? Such questions are a factor in my desire to write this book. Being different doesn't have to mean being set up for a life of hardship, but unfortunately, with the current structure of our society, that is what difference leads to, all too often. Differences are pathologized and demonized rather than cherished and supported, and that simply isn't good enough.

Another aspect to consider is that, in up to 70% of adults with ADHD, differences in executive functioning lead to difficulty in emotional regulation (Hirsch, Chavanon & Christiansen, 2019). This, of course, has knock-on effects on your relationships and ability to engage in effective interpersonal communication. Yet, emotional regulation has been proven time and time again to be a skill that can be learned. Kids grow up without effective emotional role models all the time, but they don't spend their whole lives being told they have a disorder because of it. In most cases, they recognize their bad habits and learn to do better. This type of learning can even be done formally through Dialectical Behavior Therapy (DBT), which was initially developed for psychiatric patients with severe emotional dysregulation leading to a diagnosis of Borderline Personality Disorder.

Having grown in use since its introduction, DBT has shown "significant improvements in almost all dimensions" of self-regulation in adults with ADHD (Cole et al., 2016). By focusing on learning practical self-management skills, DBT helps people with ADHD to strengthen the neural pathways associated with attention control, cognitive flexibility, and inhibitory control, all without a single organizational tool in sight. With the possibilities that this form of treatment opens, one has to wonder why modern medicine continues to repeatedly medicate neurodivergent people into a malleable, schedule-following stupor. Of course, there is nothing wrong with taking psychiatric pharmaceuticals, and they are often a crucial part of any treatment regimen just as painkillers are part of having surgery. However, it is when they become the go-to method of handling emotional regulation that problems begin. No one should have to deal with the side-effects of a higher dose of medication, when easier-to-bear, more sustainable options are possible.

Furthermore, neurodivergence isn't so simple as the overriding stereotypes of diagnosis and treatment would lead us to believe. While an inability to shift attention between tasks is part of executive dysfunction, people with ADHD tend to actually present with higher functioning in this area than their neurotypical peers. Yet, because these shifts in attention are based on the person's own desires, with inhibited impulse control, this is often mislabeled as inattention or flightiness by parents, teachers, and employers. In fact, difficulty with transitioning attention from one stimulus to another is far more indicative of autism (Otterman et al., 2019). However, because 61% of autistic people meet the DSM-5 criteria for ADHD, these traits often offset one another—at great detriment to the mental health of the neurodivergent person—and lead to the completely insufficient "high-functioning" label (Rau et al., 2020). Likewise, 65% of people diagnosed with ADHD show strong characteristic traits of ASD (Gillberg et al., 2004). However, this overlap in the comorbidity of ADHD and autism is impacted by the specific subtype of ADHD with which the person has been diagnosed, and therefore so too is the presentation of executive dysfunction altered in this way. As a result, we must understand the various presentations of ADHD and the most common comorbid conditions before we can possibly expect to find the correct methods of coping.

BRAIN BREAK:

After the fire at Paris's Notre Dame in April 2019, the cathedral was in a similar state of deterioration as it once was following the French revolution. In fact, France's often violent separation of church and state almost saw the cathedral destroyed. Victor Hugo's 1831 novel The Hunchback of Notre Dame—of course, the basis for the 1996 Disney film of the same name—was, in part, an ode to the dilapidated church. Hugo devoted two chapters of the book to describing the cathedral in its prime, and as this book gained worldwide acclaim through its various translations, the cathedral became a landmark for tourists. This, in turn, shamed the French government into restoring Notre Dame to its former glory (Bracken, 2021).

As you most likely already know, ADHD is considered to be a developmental disorder. In adults, it is diagnosed by the persistent presence of at least five symptoms relating to what is labeled as "inattention", and/or five or more symptoms of hyperactivity and impulsivity. Furthermore, for a diagnosis to be made, these symptoms must be present in two or more different social settings such as at home, work, school, or with friends. I find it frustrating that every diagnostic criterion of the condition focuses on the perceived deficits of the neurodivergent; however, for the sake of clarity and continuity, I will continue to use terminology from the DSM-5 where needed. I urge you to, please, bear with me. Understanding this terminology can be a key step in recognizing and rejecting the stereotypes placed upon you.

Interestingly, ADHD occurs along with another diagnosable condition in more than two-thirds of cases (Walitza, Drechsler & Ball, 2012). The most common of these is Autism Spectrum Disorder; however, that is merely the tip of the iceberg. Persons with ADHD are over twice as likely to develop a sleep disorder, and three times as likely to develop a tic disorder, such as Tourette's, as their neurotypical peers (Reale et al., 2017). Additionally, a study done by the Department of Health Care Policy at Harvard Medical School showed that subjects with ADHD had a roughly one in five chance of developing major depression, along with a similar likelihood of bipolar disorder. This study also showed that people diagnosed with ADHD had a 15% chance of developing a substance misuse disorder, and it is theorized that this may be the result of attempts to self-medicate when the combined effects of ADHD and a comorbidity are not fully taken into account by their treatment team (Wilens & Spencer, 2010). In each of these cases, the presence of the comorbid condition will impact the presentation of executive dysfunction.

Moreover, a diagnosis of ADHD can be further separated into three subtypes or presentations—Inattentive, Impulsive/Hyperactive, or Combined—and each of these subtypes carry their own attributes of executive dysfunction and their own likelihoods of comorbid conditions. In the case of Inattentive ADHD, the more pronounced aspects of executive dysfunction are attentional control and working memory. I must stress that this doesn't imply a "head-empty-no-thoughts" kind of existence. Instead, it means that the person will jump from one subject of hyper focus to another in quick succession. People with this presentation of ADHD are often described as "flighty" or "ditsy" as they will tend to struggle with keeping track of deadlines, remembering where they've set down their phone or keys, and staying engaged with sequentially structured tasks. This regularly results in social issues, as their forgetfulness is labeled as a lack of care. But no amount of caring can alter one's underlying cognitive abilities. People with Inattentive ADHD can't simply will their way into having a stronger working memory. Instead, they need to learn ways of coping, which can only be achieved when they are given the time and respect to explore their own thought patterns and figure out what works for them.

The presentation of the Impulsive/Hyperactive subtype of ADHD is instead linked most strongly with inhibition control. In this case, a person might be able to focus on a conversation but would struggle to wait their turn to speak. The impulse to say what they've just thought of becomes an overwhelming urge, and without development of inhibition control, they have been left powerless to fight these urges. This also shows up as blurting out answers before a question has even been completed, having trouble waiting in line, fidgeting, and being labeled a "chatter-box". Thankfully, this subtype has been noted to have a significantly lower risk of generalized anxiety and major depression when compared to the other presentations of ADHD, perhaps due to the more flexible nature of the neuroreceptors in their brains (Friedrichs, Igl, Larsson & Larsson, 2010).

Though the Impulsive/Hyperactive presentation is the rarest subtype of ADHD, this is the presentation of the condition that responds most effectively to the prescription of stimulants that is most often used in the treatment of ADHD. Prior to being diagnosed, a person with Impulsive/Hyperactive ADHD will often describe themselves as a caffeine addict. In extreme cases, this may even lead to the recreational use of amphetamines and cocaine. However, rather than the effect that these substances have on neurotypicals, people with ADHD will find themselves calmer and more focused whilst using stimulants. This is because of the effect that these drugs have on dopamine receptors in the brain, as well as their activation of key regions of the brain associated with executive functioning; the prefrontal cortex, specific subcortical regions, and the cerebellum. This results in improved inhibitory control and allows neurodivergent people to take a moment to stop and think before acting on their once overwhelming impulses. When considering potentially comorbid conditions, it's also important to note that people with both ADHD and ASD report far fewer side-effects from stimulant usage than their ADHD-only counterparts (Santosh, Baird, Pityaratstian, Tavare & Gringras, 2006). On the other hand, if a patient struggles with anxiety or motor tics, stimulants might drastically exacerbate these issues. This is yet another reason why an ADHD diagnosis should not be seen as the end of the diagnostic process.

The most common presentation of ADHD is Combined. As implied by the name, a person diagnosed with Combined ADHD will experience a combination of all types of executive dysfunction and their effects. This does not, however, mean that this is the most severe type of ADHD. There is simply more variation in the way that the condition presents itself. In fact, because hyperactivity generally decreases with age, many young people who are initially diagnosed with Impulsive/Hyperactive ADHD often discover that they have transitioned to a Combined presentation later in life (Barkely, 2010). Because there is an ebb and flow to when each form of executive functioning is the strongest or weakest in various situations, people with Combined ADHD are often labeled to be "inconsistent". Neurotypicals struggle to wrap their heads around why you can do something one day, but not the next; and therefore, when you can't do it, it is seen as coming from a place of laziness rather than a neurological block. In this form of ADHD, impaired metacognition—the ability to reflect on and analyze one's own thoughts—is also often misinterpreted as arrogance or egocentricity rather than the executive dysfunction that it truly is. These misperceptions can be incredibly damaging to your self-esteem and are not a genuine reflection of what occurs in the minds of people with ADHD.

Unfortunately, this flexibility of symptoms also appears to exacerbate the presentation of comorbid conditions in people with the Combined subtype. A 2007 study published in the *Journal of Attention Disorders* noted that individuals with the Combined presentation of ADHD had higher rates of both the instance and severity of a wide range of conditions including antisocial personality disorder, borderline personality disorder, bulimia, bipolar disorder, PTSD, and schizophrenia. Strangely, however, this increase was primarily observed in patients who were assigned male at birth (AMAB). Their assigned female at birth (AFAB) counterparts with the Combined ADHD subtype often reported less drastic differences in comorbid symptoms. Indeed, in some cases, AFAB subjects with the Combined subtype were less prone to a comorbid condition than those with other presentations of ADHD (Sprafkin, Gadow, Weiss, Schneider & Nolan, 2007).

One situation where a gender discrepancy was not noted was in the case of comorbid borderline personality disorder (BPD). In a study of over 2 million individuals, it was noted that persons with any presentation of ADHD had nearly 20 times the likelihood of a diagnosis of BPD as compared with neurotypical peers (Kuja-Halkola et al., 2018). This likely explains why DBT has proved such an effective treatment of the executive dysfunction related to inhibitory control of emotions, as DBT was initially developed by Marsha Linehan in the 1980s as a treatment for BPD. It also highlights, once again, the importance of continuing the diagnostic process beyond an initial diagnosis. The emotional dysregulation commonly associated with ADHD may, in fact, be a symptom of frequently comorbid BPD, and vice versa. If we are to adequately manage ADHD symptoms, we need to understand what is truly ADHD, and what is more likely associated with a commonly co-occurring condition. Only with this information will we be equipped to provide suitable treatment options.

Without the additional information provided by a full diagnostic sweep, it is all too easy for commonly comorbid mood disorders occurring with ADHD to be brushed off as "defensiveness" to being criticized. Likewise, a sleep disorder that should be separately diagnosed and treated can be misattributed to continued hyperactivity. Restless leg syndrome associated with iron-deficient anemia can be ignored as fidgeting. Adults with ADHD are also more likely to struggle with physiologically-caused weight gain, asthma, and chronic migraines, all of which have regularly been reportedly misattributed to some aspect of executive dysfunction (Instanes, Klungsøyr, Halmøy, Fasmer & Haavik, 2016).

It is vital that we understand where and how these conditions occur and interact with the various presentations of ADHD, in order to be capable of deconstructing the common stigmas surrounding the condition. Too often, ADHD is misunderstood and misrepresented by those who do not have the disorder. This has tremendous impacts on the lives of people with ADHD when this ignorance extend to teachers, employers, and other authority figures. Children with ADHD are often labeled as lazy or unmotivated or, on the other hand, if they have persistently good grades, a potential diagnosis of ADHD is automatically dismissed due to the stereotype that ADHD only presents in "problem" children.

In adults, struggles to remember details or obligations are frequently misconstrued as irresponsibility. This is not at all the case, and it is crucial that we disprove these boilerplate notions of what ADHD looks like. By demystifying the condition and recognizing the many ways in which it can affect people's lives, we can break down that stigma and empower people with ADHD to advocate for themselves and seek adequate support.

CHAPTER 2
ADHD Myths Debunked

Unfortunately, ADHD frequently carries a stigma attached to its diagnosis. Neurotypicals have a tendency to view the condition as merely an "excuse" for sloppiness or laziness. The fact that the symptoms of ADHD fluctuate so regularly and rapidly becomes fuel for the doubters' contempt, as they perceive this as a potential to pick-and-choose when to remain engaged in the topic at hand. Furthermore, the lack of depth in the societal conversation surrounding mental health contributes to the persistent stigmatization of psychiatric medications. Despite years of ad campaigns telling us, "It's okay not to be okay," there has been very little discussion or support of the next steps after admitting that you need assistance. All of this serves to exacerbate the negative perception of ADHD. The common media trope of college students using Adderall to stay up all night studying for a big exam has meant that medicating ADHD has somehow taken on a sinister undertone in common parlance. Combined with the fact that ADHD regularly undermines academic performance, this morphs into a belief that individuals who take their medication are somehow "cheating" their way through life.

Each of these misperceptions, along with the plethora of others surrounding ADHD, creates an environment of shame around the disorder that is completely unnecessary and unfounded. Parents will avoid seeking a diagnosis for their child—which might enable them to access vital supports—out of fear of the labels and stigmas associated with neurodivergence. Socially, and in the workplace, people with

ADHD encounter much more discrimination than their neurotypical peers which, of course, is compounded when intersecting with other marginalized identities such as race, gender, sexuality, etc. For example, in 2017, a Harvard study showed that one-third of Black Americans reported experiences of racism at their doctor's office in the past year. Similarly, members of the Global Center for Prevention and Wellness observed that clinicians spend less time with overweight patients and are more reluctant to refer these patients for important testing or consultation services (Dietz et al., 2015). These combined forms of systemic stigmatization cause one in twenty adults to be subject to a misdiagnosis at some stage in their lives (Singh et al., 2014). With this high rate of mistakes, it is strange to see healthcare practitioners continue to engage with the myths surrounding conditions, rather than attempt to keep up with the scientific facts underlying them.

Regarding ADHD, the brunt of the burden of these stigmas falls on the shoulders of girls and young women, particularly those who come from communities of color. People continue to consider ADHD to be a male disorder, and a white male disorder at that. People who are Black, Indigenous, or of another marginalized ethnic identity are more likely to be diagnosed with oppositional defiant disorder (ODD), due to the medical likelihood to view their inhibitory control issues as argumentative in the context of a white-dominated society (Ballentine, 2019). In fact, in a study of over 17,000 elementary school students, children of the global majority were, on average, 55% less likely to receive an ADHD diagnosis than their white classmates (Morgan et al., 2013). Likewise, individuals with lower socioeconomic backgrounds were also more likely to receive an ODD diagnosis than their more affluent counterparts (Loeber et al., 2000).

The effects that these biases have are a significantly underestimated risk factor in the treatment of ADHD. They affect "treatment adherence, treatment efficacy, symptom aggravation, life satisfaction, and mentally well-being of individuals affected by ADHD" (Mueller et al., 2012). Studies even suggest that the social misperceptions surrounding psychological and neurological conditions can contribute to their exacerbation, perhaps even prompting a transition in severity to full-scale psychiatric disorders (Corrigan, 2007). The extent to which this impacts individuals diagnosed specifically with ADHD is highly under-investigated, but trends seem to point towards significant repercussions in their social lives. In addition to peer rejections due to perceived "weirdness," anecdotal evidence appears to suggest that an official diagnosis of ADHD can lead to resentment from the undiagnosed. Furthermore, the effects of courtesy stigma mean that even individuals associated with the person bearing the brunt of a stigma can be negatively impacted, for no other reason than their closeness to the stigmatized person (Mueller et al., 2012).

Additionally, these stigmas come to bear against adults with ADHD significantly more often than they do with children. The stereotype of ADHD as a little boy's disorder results in increased misperceptions of adults with the condition. Even professionals and laypeople who can be quite understanding and respectful of a child with ADHD's neurodivergence are unlikely to show this same level of compassion to adults in the same circumstance.

More brutal even than these harms can be the inner violence of self-stigmatization. When continually confronted with negative criticism, it's incredibly difficult not to internalize this and perceive yourself as fundamentally flawed. Conversely, you might instead slip into a state of denial, feeling that you must have been misdiagnosed, as a way of masking your vulnerability to specifically ADHD-oriented critiques. Both of these ways of thinking about yourself inevitably cause significant psychological damage in the long term. Thus, for these reasons and more, it is vital that we tackle the ridiculous notions that surround ADHD.

BRAIN BREAK:

There are several thousand cultivars (species/types) of mango in the world, with over 1,000 of those in India alone (Litz, 2009). One of the largest single depositories of mango cultivars is in Florida, owned and operated by The United States Department of Agriculture, and even this only holds 400 of the known types of mango. The mango most often sold commercially in North America is the Haden cultivar, but the European Union and African markets tend to favor the Kent or Palmer varieties which tend to be sweeter and less fibrous.

One of the most commonly parroted misconceptions is that ADHD doesn't even actually exist. Leading ADHD media network *ADDitude* categorizes these naysayers into five groupings: the skeptics, the crusaders, the ostriches, the jokers, and the voices of doom. The skeptics deny outright that ADHD exists as a disorder. They will claim that it is a made-up diagnosis, used to medicate creative lively children into submission. Obviously, this concept of a "made-up" condition is ridiculous. What is any condition but a grouping of symptoms decided upon and commonly accepted? However, as you will see below, there are centuries of research reinforcing the validity of this particular grouping of symptoms. The brains of ADHD people are physiologically different, and that difference needs to be accepted and respected, not neglected and dismissed. While no one should need a physical difference in their neurology to gain this sort of respect, having this proof of one's differences can be a powerful tool in confronting the skeptics of the world.

The crusaders, on the other hand, might acknowledge that ADHD exists. They may even recognize that their own child might meet the diagnostic criteria for the condition. However, crusaders will denounce the use of treatments saying that they would *never* medicate their child. Similar to the ostriches of ADHD-denial, crusaders will often ignore neurodivergent differences, even in the face of significant evidence. Both crusaders and ostriches are likely to claim that they would never treat someone with ADHD differently to a neurotypical person of their age. Herein lies the problem; people with ADHD *are* different from neurotypicals of their age. Just as a colorblind approach to racism only serves to ignore the marginalization of people of color and reinforce white supremacist notions of assimilation into the white norm, ignoring the differences present in neurodivergent people only reasserts the need for them to mask until they fit the neurotypical norm. Refusing to label someone as neurodivergent doesn't somehow mean that they will no longer *be* neurodivergent; it simply cuts them off from vital supports and a sense of community and belonging. Diagnostic labels help people to know that they aren't the only ones feeling this way or dealing with these struggles. Seeing them as a source of shame reflects more about one's views on neurodivergence than the true experiences of people with ADHD. At its core, this is merely ableism disguised as care.

The final two forms of ADHD naysayers—the jokers and the voices of doom—are more overt in their ableist tactics. Jokers will shroud their distaste for ADHD with humor, accusing anyone who takes offense of being "overly sensitive." They will be the ones who most often say that ADHD is an excuse for laziness or procrastination, covering these ableist misconceptions with laughter to preemptively shut down any logical discussion of how incorrect they are. Voices of doom, on the other hand, will blatantly assert that anyone diagnosed with the condition is in store for a bleak future. They will claim that people with ADHD can't be successful; a ridiculous notion clearly refuted by the many ADHDers who have been more than capable of reaching their personal goals. They also are likely to misrepresent statistics related to the condition. For instance, some studies have shown that people with ADHD are twice as likely to have a marriage end in divorce. What voices of doom neglect to mention is that these same studies also show that this increase in the divorce rate is linked to spousal denial of ADHD rather than to the existence of the condition itself (Orlov, 2010). Unmanaged and undiagnosed ADHD can be difficult to live with, both for the person themself and for their spouse. Therefore, individuals in marriages to ADHD-deniers are more likely to have their relationship strained by the need to ignore the differences in how their brains work. It is this denial that causes resentment to build up in the relationship, as each partner blames the other for the continued effects of executive dysfunction. If voices of doom genuinely cared about the lives of people with ADHD, they would seek to break down this stigma so that these situations of mutual denial didn't occur. Instead, they prefer to demonize the neurodivergent and paint them as failures who are difficult to live with.

None of these views on the invalidity of ADHD are even remotely rooted in facts. They are instead based on ableist stereotypes and stigmas, reinforcing the myths that surround the condition rather than seeking the truth. ADHD *does* exist, and both the condition and those diagnosed with it deserve belief and respect. The facts are in their favor, it's time for society to catch up.

Since as early as 1775, medical professionals have been working to understand the variations in how we focus our attention (Weikard, 1775). In the centuries since, tens of thousands of studies surrounding what we now call ADHD have been completed. We cannot possibly justify the denouncement of the condition when scans of the brains of people with ADHD show physical differences in development as compared to neurotypical control subjects (Matthews et al., 2014). Indeed, the differences present in the cingulo-opercular, sensorimotor, frontoparietal, and occipital networks of the brains of individuals with ADHD are distinct enough to distinguish between the various subtypes of ADHD presentation with over 80% accuracy (Matthews et al., 2014). Research also shows that there are differences in the speed and age at which development occurs in the bilateral amygdala, accumbens, and hippocampus of the brains of people with ADHD (Hoogman et al., 2017). Imagine the audacity it would take to tell people with visible limb differences that their condition didn't exist! Ableists who deny the existence of ADHD should be met with the same amount of scorn for their shameless denial of physiological differences.

Furthermore, it has been proven that ADHD has a high likelihood of genetic inheritability. Where a parent has ADHD, their offspring have significantly higher chances of developing the condition. A study of close to 60,000 twins showed that, if one twin presents with ADHD symptoms, there is an 88% chance of an attention disorder diagnosis in the other twin as well (Larsson et al., 2013). With this evidence of the biological foundation for an ADHD diagnosis, it is not only foolish but completely unscientific to suggest that the condition doesn't truly exist.

Moreover, ADHD has been recognized as a legitimate diagnosis since the second edition of the DSM was published in 1968. In this edition of the manual, the condition was named as hyperkinetic impulse disorder, which was later changed to the more recognizable attention deficit disorder (ADD) in the third edition published in 1980. The condition has been confirmed to exist by the American Medical Association, the Center for Disease Control, the National Institutes of Health, and their international counterparts. Countless research bodies and medical associations are willing to stand behind the diagnosis. Any untrained layperson who thinks they have the expertise to go against the plethora of evidence in favor of the existence of ADHD needs to reflect on why they are so desperate to prove that it doesn't. Most likely, they will discover that they have quite a lot of ableism to dismantle within themselves.

The most defensive of these cynics will sometimes be willing to capitulate that okay, ADHD does exist, but will turn to another common myth to justify their distrust of the condition: it's over diagnosed! Yes, diagnostic rates of ADHD have increased in recent years. This statistical fact will lead to the assertion by some that clearly, ADHD must be diagnosed too frequently. This is *not* true. The increase in diagnoses instead reflects an increased awareness of the varying presentations of the condition. It signifies that medical professionals are improving the tools and skills by which they recognize ADHD. Additionally, increased acceptance of the presence of ADHD in persons socialized as female, and in adults who didn't receive a diagnosis in their youth, means that a larger demographic are being assessed for the condition than ever before. Therefore, even if the proportion of people receiving a diagnosis remained the same, the overall numbers of diagnoses would, of course, significantly rise. National Health Statistics Reports published by the CDC continue to show that ADHD diagnoses are clinically sound. In fact, if anything, ADHD is most likely underdiagnosed. A recent study published in the *International Journal of Psychiatry in Clinical Practice* found that, in particular, patients with psychiatric comorbidities were underdiagnosed with ADHD, and were therefore more likely to receive incomplete or inadequate treatment (Gerhand & Saville, 2021).

This underdiagnosis is compounded by assumptions about the age, sex, and race of the typical person with ADHD. The myth is, of course, that this is a disorder of young white boys. Certainly, ADHD is diagnosed in AMAB children over twice as often as their AFAB counterparts (National Center for Health Statistics, 2015). However, that doesn't mean that this gender divide is justified. A large contributor to this disparity is the myth itself. The idea that only boys have ADHD becomes a self-fulfilling prophecy, as researchers from the National Center for Gender Issues and ADHD found that 82% of teachers—the primary referrers for diagnosis—believe that ADHD is more prevalent in boys, and are therefore not on the lookout for girls presenting with similar symptoms (Quinn & Wigal, 2004). Unfortunately, this gender-driven bias in ADHD diagnoses has a devastating impact on young neurodivergent girls. Girls who go undiagnosed throughout their youth have little to no explanation for why they feel and act differently than their peers, and this contributes to self-denial or even self-hatred. Children who have been socialized as female and have undiagnosed ADHD are more likely to self-harm or attempt suicide throughout their lives, even if they receive a diagnosis in adulthood (Hinshaw et al., 2012).

Likewise, the misconception that ADHD is a children's disorder that you can "grow out of" is harmful to the health and well-being of adults who continue to struggle with the condition. A 16-year study following over 250 children into adulthood found that over 75% of people diagnosed with ADHD continue to experience symptoms of the condition as they mature (Biederman et al., 2012). Yet, the continually pushed notion that adults ought to be able to "overcome" the condition means that a large proportion of people who continue to experience those symptoms cut themselves off from treatment and try to white-knuckle their way through a society built for neurotypicals. Sadly, this can have disastrous results. Adults with ADHD have more than twice the mortality rate of their neurotypical peers, and 78% of non-disease-related deaths in adults with ADHD are a result of tragic accidents (Dalsgaard et al., 2015). A lack of support to strengthen one's inhibitory control puts ADHD adults at higher risk of car accidents, substance overdoses, and fatal violence. This does not, of course, mean that every adult with ADHD is at risk, but rather that it is important that we learn to embrace and support neurodivergence rather than deny it. Despite these risks, there is a continuing tendency by medical professionals to taper ADHD patients off of their medication by age 21 (McCarthy et al., 2009).

Counterintuitively, there is also a commonly held fallacy that prescribed medication can cure ADHD. Many people with ADHD are diagnosed, handed a prescription, and sent out into the world with no further support. What needs to be kept in mind is that medications are only one tool in the box. They are a helping hand, but they won't ever be a "cure." This mistaken belief contributes to the idea that ADHD is overmedicated. I would assert that rather than overmedicated, individuals with ADHD are under-supported. Despite common conceptions, only 62% of individuals with ADHD are treated with medication, and only a mere 47% receive any non-pharmaceutical treatment or therapy (Danielson et al., 2018). Furthermore, the stigma surrounding ADHD medications means that these average figures drop off in adulthood.

With TV shows like *Glee, Pretty Little Liars,* and *Riverdale* depicting ADHD medications as a quick fix for neurotypical teenagers to get ahead in school, anyone could be forgiven for falling into the myth of addiction and substance abuse surrounding these types of pharmaceuticals. Adults fear the impact that these drugs might have on their mental faculties, not wanting to appear high or risk the judgment associated with the use of stimulants. Parents fear allowing their children to take them in case they would prompt future substance misuse issues. However, all evidence points to the contrary. While untreated ADHD may prompt substance use in an effort to self-medicate, adequate pharmaceutical treatment significantly decreases the risk of future substance misuse or addiction. A study conducted out of Harvard Medical School and the State University of New York found, "...evidence for a significant protective effect of stimulant exposure on the subsequent development of any [substance use disorder]." This same cohort of researchers found that ADHD patients who were treated with stimulants in their youth were actually 73% less likely to develop substance use issues later in life and 72% less likely to smoke than subjects who were not treated with stimulants (Wilens et al., 2008).

Likewise, research by the Western Psychiatric Institute and Clinic stated that, " Optimal treatment of the symptoms of ADHD is the most effective way to reduce the incidence of [substance use disorders]" (Bukstein, 2007). This is attributed to two factors. Firstly, the brains of people with ADHD are physiologically different from neurotypical people. Stimulants simply don't affect these two groups in the same ways. When you have ADHD, your brain cannot use dopamine in the way the brain of a neurotypical person would. This is of concern because dopamine—along with serotonin, oxytocin, and endorphins—is responsible for transmitting positive experiences around your brain. Dopamine is the reward neurotransmitter; it provides the drive and motivation needed for productivity and creates the feel-good sensation of a job well done. Therefore, it also plays a large part in our executive function.

Many things have the potential to affect our dopamine production and use. Stress diminishes the body's ability to produce and use dopamine, which is why most people struggle to enjoy even their favorite activities when stressors are playing on their minds (Bloomfield et al., 2019). Vitamin D prompts the production of dopamine and given that vitamin D production in the body is prompted by direct sunlight on the skin, this explains why so many of us feel happier on a sunny day (Trinko et al., 2016). However, if your brain simply can't make use of this produced dopamine, as in the case for most individuals with ADHD, no amount of reducing your stress levels or sitting outside the sun will improve your executive functioning. What does help, however, are stimulants. Just as many antidepressants work by changing the way the brain makes use of serotonin, stimulants alter the way that we process dopamine. These medications slow the absorption of dopamine into the neural network, thus providing your brain with more time to make use of this vital neurotransmitter. Different stimulants achieve this in slightly different ways, and this is why not every medication will work for every person with ADHD, but 80% of ADHD patients achieve an improvement in executive functioning through the use of stimulants, and they, therefore, should not be dismissed out of hand (Kolar et al., 2008).

BRAIN BREAK:

In a counterintuitive sacrilegious turn of linguistic events, the words 'Christ' and 'grime' have the same etymological roots. Both of these words derive from the Greek *khriein* meaning "to anoint," which in turn stems from the Proto-Indo-European word *ghrēi* meaning "to rub." This etymology can also be attributed to the words 'cream' and 'grisly' (Harper, 2021).

Another nonsensical myth surrounding ADHD is that the condition is somehow caused by bad parenting. Naysayers will argue—in quite an intellectually dishonest manner—that children from low socioeconomic backgrounds are more likely to receive a diagnosis, and ridiculously equate financial standing with the ability to parent, concluding that only bad parents produce children with ADHD. This is rampant classism at its worst. I assume, dear reader, that I needn't delve into the complex nature of parenting while poor but suffice it to say that this ridiculous assertion is both insulting and factually incorrect. ADHD is not a disorder of deliberate disobedience. People with ADHD do not choose their executive dysfunction as some sort of misplaced rage at their parents.

More discipline won't ever "treat" a child with ADHD. It might force them to mask their symptoms more, but this will ultimately lead to extreme discomfort for the child. Likewise, adults with ADHD aren't rebels without a cause. Interrupting conversations, fidgeting, zoning out, or any of the myriad presentations of executive dysfunction are not calculated instances of contrariness. People with ADHD quite literally have different brains, and those differences lead to difficulty suppressing impulses. That's not a character or parenting flaw. In fact, it's not a flaw at all. It's just a difference; it's as simple as that. Genetics plays far more of a role in the development of ADHD than any aspect of one's social environment (Barkley, 2018).

Finally, and perhaps most damagingly of all, is the myth that ADHD "isn't that serious" and is being used as an excuse to be lazy. Leading ADHD expert Dr. Thomas E. Brown notes in his book, *A New Understanding of ADHD in Children and Adults: Executive Function Impairments*, that this simply isn't the case. ADHD physiologically impacts the self-management center of the brain, and as Dr. Brown states:

"ADHD often *looks* like a lack of willpower, an excuse for laziness when *it's not*...ADHD is really a problem with the chemical dynamics of the brain, it's *not under voluntary control*. ADHD symptoms are the result of neural messages in the brain not being effectively transmitted unless the activity or task is something that is really interesting."

The key misunderstanding is that people not familiar with ADHD seem to believe that you can pick and choose when executive dysfunction affects you. *You can't!* It doesn't matter whether you're trying to do boring homework, take a shower, play your favorite video game, or get ice cream out of the freezer; when executive dysfunction flares, it will prevent you from engaging even with enjoyable tasks. That isn't something that willpower can overcome. We don't tell asthmatics to "just learn to breathe better." We don't tell diabetics that they are lazy for not producing enough insulin. No one who wears glasses is ever told that they are becoming "dependent" on them or are "using them as a crutch." So, unless the neurotypicals in your life have the superhuman ability to change their own brain chemistry at will—spoiler alert, they don't—then they have zero right to tell you that you are lazy when you can't "overcome" executive dysfunction.

Like any human being, people with ADHD are lazy from time to time. We all need rest and time to recuperate from the stressors of modern life. But laziness is completely insufficient to explain ADHD symptoms. Think of the effort you need to put in every day to function in a world that's built for neurotypicals; that certainly doesn't point towards laziness. People with ADHD are some of the most determined and hardworking people I've ever met. What goes against them is neurotypical ignorance of the type of effort that neurodivergent people are required to expend every day. Because this work occurs in the privacy of their own minds, people with ADHD are continuously underestimated.

Take a look at some successful people with ADHD. Simone Biles, on top of being the most successful gymnast in history, set a powerful precedent by stepping away from the Tokyo 2020/2021 Olympics for the sake of her mental health. That takes incredible strength and resilience. A fellow Olympian, Michael Phelps, was labeled as a problem child in school but found that swimming was the perfect outlet for his ADHD-induced energy. In his 2008 autobiography he states, "In the water, I felt, for the first time, in control." Maroon 5 front man, Adam Levine, states in a PSA about owning your differences that, "When I can't pay attention, I really can't pay attention." Other celebrities with ADHD include Justin Timberlake, Solange Knowles, Richard Branson, Tim Howard, Bill Gates, and Jamie Oliver. Contrary to common belief, success with ADHD is not the exception; if geared towards an appropriate avenue, ADHD is a strength, not a weakness. People with ADHD tend to be energetic and creative risk-takers who are more than capable of thriving in an environment that suits them. But to create that environment, we need society to stop trying to diminish your talents.

So how do we go about challenging these ADHD myths in our daily lives? The first step is responding assertively to ignorant comments. Use the facts to back you up in defending your condition and protesting these vicious stereotypes. Interspersing facts with examples of your own personal journey with ADHD can be a powerful method of creating connection and opening the minds of people who feel negatively about the condition. Each person you tell your story to be likely to repeat it to others, and this will help your message spread. It has long been accepted that humans need to encounter added information three to seven times before it will cause any change in their beliefs or behaviors (Naples, 1979). Yet, by connecting this new information to someone's life experiences we can drastically shorten this absorption rate (Shiller, 2020). Therefore, our honesty about the ways we struggle with executive dysfunction can make all the difference in breaking down those stigmas surrounding ADHD. Furthermore, telling our stories creates a psychological distance from damaging self-stigmatization, giving us a sense of control, and putting us back in the driver's seat of our lives.

Another useful tactic can be to reflect a naysayer's views back at them as a question. "Why don't you believe ADHD is real?" "What specifically bothers you about the idea of ADHD?" Simply forcing someone to back up their ideas can sometimes help them to recognize that they do not have an adequate defense for their ideology. Likewise, a little bit of well-placed sarcasm can be a trigger for reassessing one's belief. "It must be nice to know more than thousands of scientists and three hundred years of research."

However, please also recognize that it is not your responsibility as a neurodivergent person to constantly be educating neurotypicals. It is important to have these kinds of conversations with your loved ones so that you can build an environment of support and respect, but continuously arguing with every misconception of your condition will only lead to burnout. Your primary goal needs to be your own mental well-being.

Thankfully, not as much of this work is the responsibility of the neurodivergent in recent years. The U.S. Senate assigned the second Wednesday of every September from 2004 onwards to be National ADHD Awareness Day. This has since expanded to an international ADHD awareness month every October. I hope that these continued initiatives can help us to enlighten the world on the truth of ADHD rather than the stereotypes. In the meantime, you need to prioritize your own life. Learning to accept and manage your condition is the most important fight of all.

CHAPTER 3
Beginning to Heal — Accepting and Embracing ADHD

Dealing with a new diagnosis of any kind is never easy. Coping with a diagnosis of a condition that is so stigmatized, in the way that ADHD is, is even harder. Hardest of all, is being aware that you most likely have such a condition but are without the means or privilege to access a professional diagnosis. Regardless of what position you find yourself in, I hope that this chapter grants you the space to explore and understand your feelings about your neurodiversity. Learning to accept yourself is a life-long journey, but as the oft-quoted Lao Tzu said, "The journey of a thousand miles begins with a single step." This is that step.

When initially coming to terms with a possible or probable diagnosis of ADHD, the foremost emotions can often be relief and optimism. It is a blessing to finally have a title to put on your experiences. You now know that you are not alone in these feelings. What is more, you no longer feel the need to internalize the insults that may have been flung at you; that you're lazy, ungrateful, or unmotivated. You can offer yourself some compassion in the knowledge that your executive dysfunction is not a character flaw, but a difference in your neurological wiring. This, in turn, can help you to build your self-confidence as you let go of invalid internal criticisms. Research shows that adults with official diagnoses of ADHD are, "...able to defeat unnecessary negative emotions and self-blame" (Fleischmann &

Fleischmann, 2012). The emotional freedom that this understanding and self-compassion can grant should not be underestimated. It is a powerful prompt for change in self-esteem and willingness to advocate for oneself.

Discovering a diagnosis also opens the pathway to treatments and support systems. Joining forums dedicated to discussing experiences of ADHD can help you to develop a sense of community and find a place of belonging that you may not have felt you had before. Having a professional diagnosis not only means having access to medication, if you so choose, but also being able to apply for accommodations in your workplace or educational institution. Even just having a better understanding of what's going on with you can help immensely as it enables you to seek out relevant information and coping techniques. Thinking that you are a chronic procrastinator will lead you to motivational speakers and organizational techniques but knowing that you have ADHD can help you to respect your moments of inertia, embrace rest, and maneuver your life to work around the ebbs and flows of your energy rather than forcing yourself into burnout by attempting to "push through."

However, this euphoric relief is rarely the only emotional response to a diagnosis. As you become more cognizant of the many stigmas and stereotypes associated with ADHD, you may feel a sense of denial. You may not want to be associated with this label and all its infamy. If you receive your diagnosis quite spontaneously, rather than as a result of your own research and request for an assessment, it may come as quite a shock. You might not necessarily recognize how faulty a lot of the common parlance surrounding ADHD truly is. You might laugh that you aren't a hyperactive little boy, you just need help knuckling down at work. If you accept the diagnosis superficially, perhaps you will treat it as merely a title, disregarding the potential benefits of viewing this label as a jumping-off point for beginning treatment.

Many newly diagnosed people with ADHD swear that they will never take medications for it, being caught up in the misguided pill-shaming phenomenon that so often occurs. The shift in one's sense of self that can follow the recognition of probable ADHD can be so frightening that anything to do with the diagnosis—even the aspects of ADHD and its treatments that can be vastly beneficial—are brutally shoved away, much to their own detriment.

For many people who aren't diagnosed until adulthood—my own sister included—there can also be an accompanying sense of anger. You might rage at God or the universe for not making you "like everybody else." There can be a sense of self-blame that you somehow should have foreseen this diagnosis and preemptively "overcome" it as if that were even possible. However, most often, looking back can cause the realization of how obvious your struggles with executive dysfunction should've been to the people around you, and in particular those adults that had authority over you and a duty of care towards you. At that stage, it's hard not to feel resentful towards those authority figures in your life that should have helped you come to terms with your differences instead of admonishing you for the ways that they played out. Family members who blamed you for undone chores, teachers who scolded you for fidgeting or staring out the window, every painful memory reminds you of a chance that you could've accessed this diagnosis—and therefore, the treatments and supports that accompany it—sooner.

When confronted with the memories of those missed opportunities for clarity, it's hard not to grieve for the younger you that blamed themself for their struggles. You can't help but wonder, *who would I be now if I had been understood and supported then?* If you had had accommodations in school, perhaps your grades would've gotten you into a different college. If your family had respected your differences, maybe you wouldn't carry so much self-blame. If you had had an explainable reason to give when you made a social misstep, such as cutting someone off during a conversation, you might not have lost friends or frustrated colleagues. The fact that ADHD brains process emotion differently can also mean that this sense of sorrow feels utterly overwhelming.

In some cases, this sense of grief for the past also extends into grief for the future. Doom and gloom thinking seeps in, and if neurotypical norms were something that you had always worked towards, coming to terms with your divergence from these norms may be a painful process. You might feel that the goals you had set for yourself are now unreachable in the knowledge that your brain is fundamentally different from that of a neurotypical. The disappointment in knowing that although various treatments can help, there is no definitive cure, can feel like receiving a life sentence. It might all feel like too much to handle. Your perception of your past is often unalterably changed, but you don't have to feel stuck in this apocalyptic view of your future.

So often, science fiction discussions turn to the potential effects of time travel. We fear traveling to the past and having our minor actions vastly disturb the version of the present that we came from. But how often do we consider the ways in which our actions in the present can drastically affect our futures?

That's why the acceptance of ADHD is so vital. It quite genuinely has the power to change the paths of our lives. Acceptance empowers you to embrace your differences, build up support networks for when you need them, and find strength in your unique characteristics, working with rather than against your neurodivergence. Acceptance is not a one-and-done emotion though. Unfortunately, the events of life have a tendency to plunge us back into the cycle of grief now and again. When we accidentally slip into an old coping mechanism or are once again admonished for something outside of our control, our emotions flash back to that misunderstood child, and this brings about a whole new round of the grieving process. Consequently, acceptance needs to be a continued effort to embrace the idea of yourself as an individual with ADHD. Rather than seeing your neurodivergence as a flaw, you aim to see it as simply a part of you. Managing your symptoms no longer means engaging in a self-denying chore that feels necessary to fit in, and instead, it involves the act of self-compassion and self-respect. Managing symptoms doesn't mean covering them up; it means finding a path to a version of your life that you are content with.

Likewise, acceptance isn't about complacency or indifference towards your ADHD. It's *certainly* not a case of writing yourself off as a lost cause. Instead, it's a process of working with your strengths and challenges and learning to approach your condition from a place of collaboration rather than reprimand. It's about knowing that it's okay to seek out the resources that can grant you the capacity to build a life you are fulfilled by. As I mentioned in the previous chapter, we wouldn't ever shame someone with vision difficulties for needing glasses. You shouldn't blame yourself for needing a little support when you're struggling either.

BRAIN BREAK:

In Switzerland, it is illegal to keep many specific animals—including guinea pigs—on their own, to prevent them from becoming lonely.

A 2003 piece of legislation was enacted following advice from the Federal Food Safety and Veterinary Office which warned that social animals should not be subjected to solitary confinement. This act has been amended various times since to include animals such as, but not limited to, guinea pigs, mice, gerbils, chinchillas, quails, parakeets, canaries, anteaters, and wolves (Tierschutzverordnung (TSchV) 455.1, 2018).

Bonus fact: This same piece of legislation also outlaws forcing domestic poultry to wear glasses or contact lenses. I have no idea why that needed to be specified, but I guess Swiss chickens better hope they have 20/20 vision!

You are a human being, and like any other member of our species, you will need help from time to time. That's okay. No one can possibly handle everything on their own. Humans are social creatures. It's important to know that this need for support is a representation of your humanity, not any signifier of weakness or "disorder." You are so much more than a list of symptoms in your medical charts. A diagnosis can be scary, but it's also the key to unlocking a world of understanding. Perhaps you've spent a lifetime being compared to your neurotypical classmates or siblings, and always feeling that the metrics for this comparison left you with the short end of the stick. Society might focus on your challenges, but that doesn't mean that you have to follow suit. It doesn't mean that you yourself need to ignore your talents. Forcing yourself to be "normal" is never the path to fulfillment. You can reach your goals by embracing your true self. It's okay if that means that your methods of reaching those goals are different.

But how do we go about aiming for this level of acceptance? An incredibly useful starting point is to educate yourself. Reading this book, for instance, is a great step. Might I also recommend taking to the internet and finding other people who also have ADHD. Reading the stories of people with similar struggles can be incredibly validating. Knowing that you aren't alone in this experience somehow makes it easier to bear; I guess a problem shared truly is a problem halved. Additionally, this community can help you to find reliable sources for further research. Sadly, a lot of ableism exists online, so try to avoid falling into the pit of despair surrounding the myths of ADHD. Learning more about ADHD from reputable sources can help you to understand that you are not to blame for the ways that your symptoms present. This type of research can also help with the recognition that you have more control in your life than you might be inclined to think. By letting go of the effort to live up to neurotypical goals, you can expend your energy more effectively elsewhere.

Support groups can be a powerful tool to help you process these heavy thoughts. Similarly, counseling can be an excellent opportunity to bounce your thoughts off of a professional sounding board. However, if you decide to go this route, it is vital that your counselor be well-versed in the truths of ADHD and not end up reinforcing ableist stereotypes in your mind. It's okay to ask questions of a counselor in your first couple of sessions and scope out their experience with ADHD patients. Ultimately, if they aren't capable of providing you with the support that you need, it's better to find this out right off the bat. Even in countries with socialized healthcare, where counselors are generally assigned to patients rather than chosen, you almost always have the right to request to be placed with someone else if your first counselor doesn't feel like a good fit.

When you have found the right person to help you on this journey to acceptance, you may decide on some key areas of focus for your emotional energy. One of these might be accepting that your brain chemistry is the way it is, without labeling that difference as good or bad. You are not broken, and you do not need to be fixed. If you are inclined to have these sorts of thoughts, it is vital that you work to understand why so that you can effectively dismantle these notions. Many people will find that they have deep-seated, internalized ableism and sadism surrounding any form of neurological or psychological differences. Under various court rulings, ADHD is classified as a disability, and if this terminology makes you uncomfortable, you may need to evaluate why you see disability as a bad word. It is so easy for ableist media tropes to infiltrate our minds, but when these concepts are infringing on our ability to accept ourselves, they are also often contributing to the marginalization of others, and that is *not* okay.

Though ADHD should not be the main feature of how you identify yourself, it is important that you learn to acknowledge the ways that it impacts your day-to-day life. By definition, a disability is any condition that makes it more difficult for you to engage in day-to-day tasks or interact with the world around you. In this context, ADHD fits the brief. Just as disabled people with mobility issues might need a walker or a wheelchair, people with ADHD might need certain aids to help them through their day, and that's absolutely okay. Under the social model of disability, the factor that makes someone disabled is not the medical condition itself, but rather the attitudes and structures in society that create inaccessibility for anyone outside the neurotypical, able-bodied norm. Society isn't built for people with ADHD. That is not your fault, and neither is your condition. You are not damaged, you are diverse. Society's reluctance to make room for that is not a reflection on who you are as a person.

We're constantly bombarded with the message that our self-worth ought to be tied up in our productivity. A person's job and their income have sadly become representative of their perceived contribution to society. This kind of materialistic thinking can be incredibly detrimental to people with ADHD, who often find themselves struggling with the repetition involved in many forms of employment. Allow me to state point-blank that you have intrinsic worth. Your productivity, or lack thereof, is not a reflection of who you are, or what you mean to the people around you. ADHD is not a weakness of willpower or a moral failure. Different does *not* mean damaged. Disabled does not mean expendable. As one adult with ADHD, Christine from Winnipeg, put it, "My house is standing and functioning. My family is fed. My son is being educated, and my husband loves me. No fixing needed here" ("I Don't Need to Be Fixed! Epiphanies of Self-Acceptance from Adults with ADHD", 2020).

BRAIN BREAK:

Fredrick the Great—king of Prussia from 1740 to his death in 1786—pulled off one of the greatest feats of reverse psychology of all time, and it all had to do with potatoes!

Despite potatoes now being the world's fourth most popular crop, when they were introduced to Prussia Frederick's subjects scorned potatoes for years stating, "The things [potatoes] have neither smell nor taste, not even the dogs will eat them, so what use are they to us?" In order to encourage their cultivation, Frederick the Great ordered the planting of a royal potato garden which was to have guards stationed around it at all times. However, these guards were explicitly instructed to be bad at their jobs. Frederick wanted thieves to covet the tuber, and by framing them as a strictly royal food item he ensured that public craving for potatoes increased drastically. This clever marketing scheme led to farmers prioritizing the potato, and effectively doubled the production of calories per acre from farms in Prussia which in turn allowed for the population growth that eventually spurred industrialization.

In addition to being a master of agricultural deception, Frederick the Great was also an LGBTQ+ icon. After being defeated on the battlefield he stated, "Fortune has it in for me; she is a woman, and I am not that way inclined." (Howell, 2020)

Acceptance and Commitment Therapy (ACT) is a powerful tool for radically embracing hard-to-swallow truths about yourself and your life, as is so often sadly the case for people with ADHD who have been listening to ableist criticisms their entire lives. Initially used as a psychotherapeutic technique for patients with chronic or terminal diagnoses, ACT is continuously expanding to be used in accepting more and more aspects of day-to-day life. This form of therapy focuses on the ability to sit with uncomfortable experiences. Its foundations are seated firmly in the stoic philosophy of ancient Greece whose founder Seneca stated, "We are more often frightened than hurt; and we suffer more from imagination than from reality" (Seneca, 054 AD). By acknowledging the ways in which our perceptions can distort our experiences, ACT enables us to accept the underlying truth of a situation. Focusing on our awareness of ourselves, our beliefs, and our surroundings empowers us to view the aspects of a given circumstance that are in or out of our control, and to act in a manner that reflects our true desires and values.

You should not have to change or "fix" yourself. ADHD is not a diagnosis of disaster. Likewise, acceptance doesn't mean loving every aspect of your condition in some pseudo-euphoric form of toxic positivity. Contrary to the popular usage of the word "stoic," this philosophy does not embody indifference or stagnation in the face of adversity. Neither does its modern therapeutic usage as part of ACT. Some parts of ADHD do suck, there's no getting around that fact. But that doesn't mean that you are doomed to a life of misery and underachievement. By using ACT skills to help you with recognizing and accepting those symptoms that most frustrate you, you can empower yourself to explore that frustration. Why do those aspects of your symptoms irritate you the most? What, in your environment, exacerbates the presentation of those symptoms? What changes can you make to the context of your life to ease this self-criticism? However, none of these questions can be answered without you first becoming open to an honest internal conversation with yourself about the truth of how ADHD affects you and your life. Only then can you get to grips with what you can and can't change about your journey through life, and how you can adjust your environment to support you through your ADHD.

If you have the means to privately seek treatment and support, an ADHD coach can be a useful companion on this journey of self-acceptance and understanding. These aren't the kind of coaches that make you run laps of a football field until you pass out. Similar to a counselor, an ADHD coach can help you to discuss and discover your personal strengths and weaknesses. However, the main advantage of this type of coaching is its ADHD orientation. ADHD Coaches are professionally trained in the ways that this specific form of neurodiversity affects your thinking. Therefore, they won't recommend all the many organizational techniques that you already know are bound to fail. They understand that executive dysfunction is not a time-management issue or a lack of motivation and can help you to make use of your strengths and manage your weaknesses at your own pace and without judgment. They employ a collaborative approach to help you develop systems that work for you and can be a valuable source of praise that will stimulate your dopamine usage. This can then gradually develop into an internalized improvement in self-esteem, confidence, and overall well-being (Ahmann et al., 2017).

Just as with counseling, however, it is crucial to find a coach that is the right fit. It's perfectly okay to question a potential coach around their qualifications, specializations, experience, workload, and fees before agreeing to become their client. Some coaches may have previously worked exclusively with children and might not be adequately equipped to help you to tackle adult responsibilities and obligations. Similarly, some coaches work primarily with employed business people, and if you are self-employed or a homemaker you might find their approach to be too obedience- and productivity-oriented.

Moreover, some coaches take a little-and-often approach, preferring to meet with you frequently for short periods of time, and this may either suit you perfectly or be completely incompatible with your schedule. Whatever your personal needs, if you believe that coaching would be a good choice for you, I urge you to persevere with finding the correct person to help you on that journey. Some ADHD support groups even incorporate a coaching element, either through hiring a coach as a group leader or through implementing some form of mentorship program between group members. This might be a more informal— and cheaper—option if one-to-one coaching doesn't seem like the right choice for you.

Whatever choice you make of how you want to pursue acceptance is your own. It's okay to make the wrong decision and change tracks down the road. The important part is to grant yourself the freedom to make a start with this process. This conscious effort to acknowledge the role that neurodivergence plays in your life prevents the all too common imposter syndrome from taking hold. Without this self-compassion, you might feel as though you have somehow misled or fooled your doctors into giving you the diagnosis, even if you can logically acknowledge your presentation of ADHD symptoms. You can dismiss your own struggles with phrases like, "not that bad," and further hinder your progress, not only towards self-compassion but towards your more tangible goals as you get caught in the headlights of perfection paralysis. Even medicated individuals, who have found a significant easing of their symptoms through their use of medication, are prone to self-doubt if they aren't actively working towards accepting themselves as an individual with ADHD. This is a particular risk of returning to these thoughts of self-denial if you were skilled at masking your symptoms in your youth. Without failing grades, or school reports noting distractibility, it's easy for those niggling thoughts to creep in. *Well, if I coped back then, why can't I cope now? Clearly, I must not have ADHD if my parents and teachers didn't pick up on it?*

When these doubts sneak up on you it's crucial to ask: *Was I really coping? How much harder than my classmates did I have to work to maintain those standards? Were my high grades just in the classes that interested me and therefore sparked my dopamine response? Though I may have appeared to be flourishing academically, how was I doing emotionally? Is it sustainable to ask myself to maintain my childhood standards now that I have adult responsibilities to contend with?* Being labeled as "gifted" as a child can cause as much self-blame and shame as being labeled as "difficult." Neither label gives an adequate impression of a child's inner experience, and both are likely to hold a child responsible for the arbitrary standards set by a neurotypical society. As an adult, you have a responsibility to honor your inner truth. Identifying and owning your ADHD is a part of that truth.

You deserve to feel good about yourself. You deserve to respect your limits and be able to praise yourself. Perhaps by now you have spent years beating yourself up for your ADHD, so let me ask you: Did it work? Does blaming and shaming ourselves ever work? I can certainly testify that I have never actually managed to motivate myself through meanness. If anything, my inner criticisms have sometimes prevented me from making any effort for fear of failure.

It's time to take a new perspective. It's time to be compassionate towards your differences. In our relationships with others, we sometimes have to take a deep breath and remind ourselves of all the reasons that we love them in order to stop ourselves from blowing up when they frustrate us. We need to remember to apply this skill to ourselves as well. Remember all of the amazing experiences you never would have had were it not for your ability to take risks. Focus on the way that others love you for your random questions and intriguing conversations. Whatever your strengths are, accept them. Whatever your challenges are, accept them too. They are all a part of you and will each help you to determine how to take steps towards a more fulfilling version of your life.

Once you have come to terms with the many facets of yourself and your diagnosis, you can start to put this understanding to good use. By recognizing your strengths, you can make the most of them, and by acknowledging the areas of life in which you are more prone to stumble, you can build a safety net for yourself so that these missteps no longer feel like failures. As Mikella from Alabama put it, "I lived my whole life knowing I was different but not understanding why. Learning about ADHD in adults helped me understand why I thought and approached problems differently. I always understood me, (I live in here!) but I didn't understand how to bridge a gap I couldn't see. Being diagnosed let me see the gap and build the bridge" ("I Don't Need to Be Fixed! Epiphanies of Self-Acceptance from Adults with ADHD", 2020).

CHAPTER 4
Surround Yourself with Support

Accepting ADHD and the role that it plays in your life necessarily involves some changes in the perspective that you take on life. This altered view often impacts the choices that you make in how you want to live your life, which can be quite a harrowing experience, particularly for those of us who have previously been very set in our ways. Therefore, having a strong support system—both internally, and in your network of family, friends, and other neurodivergent people—will help you to weather these changes effectively and build the kind of life that you want.

Official support groups can be an accessible introduction to this type of support network. Because they are available both in-person and online, there is a wide variety of options to choose from according to your own schedule and accessibility needs. While local groups can help you meet like-minded people who live nearby and build friendships in your neighborhood, they may not meet often enough or in a location accessible enough to be of true use to you. On the other hand, the wide range of online groups available means that you can pop into an international meeting at any time of the day or night when you feel up to it, but you may miss out on the closeness prompted by a more consistent approach. The choice is entirely yours, and even if you make one choice and find that it's not right for you, don't let that stop you from exploring other avenues. The association of Children and Adults with Attention-Deficit/Hyperactivity Disorder (CHADD) has a US-wide network of affiliates, as well as an online forum dedicated to adults with ADHD, and can be a useful place to start connecting with other people who share similar experiences of the condition. Likewise, most social media platforms have dedicated groups and hashtags that can be a valuable source of information and friendship.

These sorts of connections continue to be one of the most useful and underutilized tools in the road to managing any form of neurodivergence. The true experts in any condition aren't the neurotypical people that have studied it formally in a clinical environment; they are the people who live with and manage the condition every day of their lives. A shockingly wide-reaching amount of practical information about ADHD is stored in the minds of people just like you; it's simply a matter of reaching out. Whether that's through a formal support group, a Facebook group, a hashtag on Twitter, or even starting your own "Neurodivergent Natter" group in your local community hall, these networks are an opportunity to learn that you aren't alone. They offer a safe space and a chance to hear the stories of people who are also finding their way through a neurotypical-oriented society; to pick up tips and tricks on how to ride out that rollercoaster; to find shoulders to cry on and companions to laugh with. A sense of belonging is a key need for human psychological well-being, and just being part of one of these groups can help ease the tension of learning and accepting who you truly are.

Beyond these types of communities, it is also crucial that you have support from the communities of which you are already a part. Your friends and family, sadly, might be slow to understand this need though, and that is why more formalized support groups can be a worthwhile stopgap in the meantime. As we saw in Chapter 2, a great many misconceptions surrounding ADHD seep into the collective unconscious and, as a result, your loved ones may unfortunately have some stigmas of their own that they need to dismantle. Being witness to this process—and the potential stubbornness against change that often accompanies it—can be painful. These may be the same people who have spent years ridiculing you for something that wasn't actually under your control, and to accept your diagnosis will mean admitting that they were wrong to treat you like that. This realization can often be too much all at once and they may slip into bad habits, once again mocking you for your ADHD, feeling that this projection onto you will protect them from the knowledge of their own failure to respect and support you. While this is—to some degree—understandable, it is not acceptable, and you are well within your rights to continue to set boundaries around the kind of behavior you will and won't accept.

You deserve the support of your loved ones. You shouldn't have to fight to be respected or loved. But if you do, the first step is often an internal one. If you haven't yet processed and accepted that you have ADHD, this self-doubt can be used as ammunition against you. But if, on the other hand, you feel confident, secure, and self-compassionate in the knowledge that you are different and that's okay, you won't need the validation of others and will feel more at ease in advocating for yourself. Of course, that's easier said than done, but stick with it. Don't blame yourself if your loved ones do latch onto any doubts, you might be feeling about your ADHD, and simply remind yourself that those criticisms are not based on the truth. In *Chapter 6: Protecting Your Progress*, we'll take a look at some key facts you can use to reassure yourself through these difficult situations.

It's also advantageous to have a selection of information about ADHD to either quote to your loved ones or direct them towards for their own further research. Just as educating yourself can open your mind to the wide reality of ADHD outside of the narrow stereotyping, education is a valuable means to engaging your family and friends in a discussion about your neurodivergence. Sharing your experiences, as well as the experiences of others with ADHD, will allow your loved ones to recognize the commonalities and differences in the multitude of ways that ADHD can affect one's life. At the end of this chapter, I have included a section specifically geared towards the non-ADHD members of your family and friends, which can be handed to them to read so that you don't have to do all the convincing alone. A short piece like this can often be a stepping stone to self-driven research, and I hope that you will find it helpful in garnering the support and understanding that you deserve from your loved ones.

This support can truly change the way you feel about your interactions with the world as a person with ADHD. Being surrounded by people who understand your symptoms and respect your limitations becomes a positive feedback loop. You exude self-acceptance, so your loved ones learn to accept you. They respect you, and you consequently learn to respect yourself. You understand and set boundaries based on your limitations, and they help you to recognize when you may be taking too much onto your plate. This network provides vital encouragement through your struggles, invaluable praise through your triumphs, and sometimes even a little tough love when you aren't effectively working to meet your own needs. Most importantly, they never lead with shame or chastisement. They never make you feel like a burden, or an idiot, or a lay-about. They don't *ever* accuse you of using your diagnosis as an excuse. Any person that does these sorts of things needs to educate themselves on the truths of ADHD, and it is okay to set hard boundaries with them until they follow through on that need. If they refuse to follow through on unlearning their bigotry, it may even be necessary to minimize or end your contact with them for the sake of your own safety.

You shouldn't ever have to feel like a second-class citizen in your relationships or family. You have seen throughout the previous chapters that misconceptions of ADHD are common, but that doesn't mean that it's somehow excusable for your loved ones to level these myths at you as an indictment of your character. Misinformation is an opportunity for education, but no adult should expect you to carry out that education for them. It is okay to decide that you need your mental health more than you need a given bigoted friend or family member. In fact, this can even sometimes be the wake-up call that they needed to address their problematic behavior. You deserve respect, and you have a right to leave any environment that doesn't provide you with that.

 BRAIN BREAK:

The smell of rubbing alcohol—and therefore, many hand sanitizers— is more effective at treating nausea and vomiting than the most commonly used antiemetic medication, ondansetron (Lindblad et al., 2018). When ondansetron costs $4/pill, and the smell of rubbing alcohol is twice as effective, I think I know what I'll be choosing the next time I feel nauseous.

With the right people surrounding you, you don't need to feel on edge or constantly fearful of slipping up and committing a social faux pas. Supportive people are capable of understanding that you will sometimes miss deadlines, arrive late to meetings, or zone out mid-conversation sometimes, and will not use your symptoms as a cause for judgment. They know that cutting you some slack will be far more productive in the long term than harsh admonishment. They will understand that rest in and of itself can be productive; that when you say you can't do something, you truly can't; that executive dysfunction is not laziness.

Moreover, the right people will share in your triumphs. They will be a valuable source of dopamine-boosting praise and affection. In addition to sharing their compassion when you are struggling, they will recognize the small personal victories like realizing you need to go to the bathroom before you're bursting, beginning to interrupt someone and stopping yourself, and remembering to eat. They don't tease you for treating these as achievements. They appreciate the hard work and self-awareness that goes into fighting executive dysfunction, and they can help you to develop both of these. One such way that your loved ones can support you is by engaging in "body doubling" with you. Body doubling is simply sitting with you while you engage in a task. They won't talk or help you with the task, as this could be distracting or condescending. Instead, they will just keep you company. This simple action boosts your dopamine production and creates an instant sense of self-motivation and willingness to initiate the task. It can also help you to form a routine for boring mundane tasks. In exactly the way that many people have a gym buddy to motivate them to stick to a workout regime, having a monthly or weekly appointment when your friend will sit with you while you pay your bills will help you to adhere to tasks where time limits can't be avoided. Whether body doubling is done in person, or through an online video chat platform, it is equally beneficial and can help you to accomplish boring tasks such as laundry, studying, cooking, journaling, catching up on emails, and anything else you find under stimulating yet necessary.

Overall, supportive people accept you for exactly who you are, and while they will help you through the changes that you want to make, they will never force you into feeling like you need to change. The great thing is, you don't need a small army of these people, just one can make all the difference (Cox, 2019). This person will make you feel valued, not for what you can do in spite of your ADHD, but for who you are because of it. Your insomnia won't be a "failure to keep a schedule," it will be an amazing opportunity to go down Wikipedia wormholes and hyper focus on whatever interests you. They will remind you of your ingenuity, your resilience, your humor, whatever makes you, you. Most importantly, they will remind you of your lovability. They will remind you that the people that have misjudged you for the ways that your ADHD presents itself were _wrong_; even when they might have once been prone to that same misjudgment themself.

It may take time for your loved ones to come around to this way of thinking, but if you feel that they are willing to learn, it's important to keep challenging their misconceptions—though as I mentioned, not at the cost of your mental health; if your emotional well-being is suffering from repeated conflicts about these stigmas, then you need to walk away. People respond well to stories. As children, we learn a lot of our morality from the experiences of fictional characters, and how telling your own stories can invoke this learning mindset in others. Beginning with, "I can see why you might believe this, but in my experience…" you set the stage for a learning opportunity without any need for direct confrontation. Likewise, "That's a common ADHD trope in the media, but in my experience of living with the condition… Furthermore, science has shown…" will set you up for a civilized discussion about the facts of ADHD.

In some cases, if you are attending a counselor or ADHD coach, it can be useful to invite a loved one to sit in on one of your sessions. Having the affirming presence of a trained professional in the room can help you to stand your ground when speaking to your friend or family member, and having that person witness that this specific professional agrees with your diagnosis can help them overcome any lingering doubts or denial; sometimes, the theoretical knowledge of a diagnosis is too conceptual to fully sink in.

In the case of a family member—and in particular, a parent or guardian—it can also be helpful to remind them that you don't blame them for your ADHD. While you may harbor some resentment if you were diagnosed later in life, it is best to leave this aspect of the conversation to one side until your family member is more accepting of the diagnosis as a whole. Because of the common myth that ADHD is caused by poor parenting, many guardians can perceive the disclosure of an ADHD diagnosis to be an attack on their character. This can cause a defensive reaction which can escalate to the overall denial of the condition. Let them know that ADHD is just something you have, not something that was "inflicted on" you, that the condition is no one's "fault," and that ADHD does not mean that something is wrong with you, simply that your brain works differently. Remind them that you're only asking for their continued love and support, not an apology.

Without sufficient understanding of ADHD, it can feel like a curse upon your brain, and this can be the way that others misperceive it. Your support network should help you to recognize the ways in which you can counteract these challenges, as well as the ways that ADHD can sometimes feel like a blessing. People with ADHD tend to thrive in busy environments where they have many things drawing their focus. For this reason, they make excellent bartenders, nurses, and childcare workers. When you adapt and work with your brain, ADHD can help you excel beyond neurotypical norms. It is only when you attempt to crush yourself into submission to these norms—such as is demanded by so much of the education system—that the condition feels extremely overwhelming. Your support network, whether a formal group or a favorite family member, should help you remember this. They love you for who you are. As the saying goes, those who matter don't mind, those who mind don't matter.

SUPPORTING YOUR ADHD LOVED ONE

This section of the book is for the friends and family members of a person with ADHD, so if that is you, thank you for caring about them enough to read this. There are so many misconceptions around ADHD, and while we won't have the time to challenge them all in this small section, I hope to give you a crash course in the condition, and how you can be of help to your loved one.

One vitally important thing that you can do is educate yourself about ADHD, and the fact that you are reading these words already shows that you are up to that challenge. Another crucial aspect is to listen to your loved one. ADHD is a complex condition that affects each individual in a myriad of ways. Your loved one will be truly grateful if you can open up and listen to the ways that the condition has impacted their life, specifically. They have been living with this condition their entire life—regardless of if or when they received a diagnosis—and this truly does make them the expert. Please, respect their expertise. They know their own brain and life better than anyone. Your compassion and willingness to listen can make a huge difference in how they perceive themselves, and their ability to cope and manage their symptoms.

Beyond this kind of active listening, some general education on the issues surrounding ADHD can also be remarkably helpful. It shows your loved one that you care enough to do the research yourself. Some topics to begin with can be learning the variety of ways that ADHD can present itself, the difficulties it can pose, the strengths it can endow, and the fact that none of this is within your loved one's control. Their brain is wired differently, that's not a fault or a flaw, simply a fact. Understanding the ways that this neurodivergence impacts their life can help you to have patience with them when their executive dysfunction is presenting particularly strongly. Executive dysfunction—the key cohort of symptoms in individuals with ADHD—impacts one's working memory, sense of time, self-awareness, impulse control, emotional regulation, and motivation. People with ADHD don't mean to miss deadlines, and they don't undervalue your time when they are late to your plans; they have executive dysfunction and that influences their ability to keep track of these kinds of time-oriented tasks. Likewise, they aren't lazy or procrastinating when they don't engage with a given task; their brain quite genuinely will not let them. No amount of willpower or cajoling can change that, but guilt-free rest can. You can be a key element in helping them avoid the all too common forms of self-shame and blame that can seep in when they need a break.

As hard as it can be to hear, you will also need to take the time to recognize how the presentation of ADHD has impacted *you* and your relationship with your loved one. While it is definitely important to provide them with your respect and support, you shouldn't be overextending yourself to "compensate" for their executive dysfunction and should protect your own mental health as well. Recognize the role that you have been playing in your loved one's life. This might be the overprotective parent/sibling role, where you micromanage their life to help them avoid mistakes, it might be the high-school-football-coach-esque role of shouting at them to get their act together or, more likely, it's somewhere in between. Assess whether this is appropriate to your relationship to the person, their age, and the true nature of ADHD. Evaluate whether what you've been asking of them is truly within the realms of possibility, and whether what you've been expecting of yourself can be sustainable in the long term.

Accepting the aspects of your loved one's condition that are outside of their control can help you support them through changes that are *within* their control. One of the most important aspects of managing

ADHD is working *with* the condition rather than against it, and this can mean making changes to their environment. One such technique can be "body doubling." Body doubling involves sitting with a person with ADHD while they complete a task. Even via an online platform such as Zoom or Facetime, this method of keeping your loved one company can make a massive difference to their ability to engage with the task. There's no need to speak, or do the task with them—in fact, you can even work on your own thing at the same time—simply having another person there is a powerful motivator and source of focus for a person with ADHD. Recent research out of Northeastern Illinois University has shown the efficacy of this simple technique in providing structure and accountability for students with ADHD (Jackson, 2021).

This technique is mirrored in the concept of "parallel play" associated with autism—another form of neurodivergence that commonly co-occurs with ADHD. Parallel play involves being "alone together." Rather than focusing on a specific task, each person engages with their own hobby, in each other's company but separately. This can also be helpful for individuals with ADHD who struggle to engage with hobbies under the idea that their energy should be put towards something "useful" when they have energy.

People with ADHD are often regularly admonished for their symptoms, and this is incredibly detrimental to their mental health and overall well-being. Though it might seem helpful to encourage them to meet social norms, which you might see as beneficial to their work or educational lives, this should be avoided at all costs. Masking—the repression of neurodivergent traits—is strongly negatively correlated with neurodivergent well-being and is thought to be a large contributor to shorter lifespans in people with autism and ADHD. If you want to support your loved one, remind them of their strengths. Show them that they don't need to change to earn your love or respect; they already have it.

Dealing with a condition that is misunderstood by the world to be synonymous with hyperactive little boys can be tough on anyone, including those who actually do or did once fit the stereotype. ADHD is so much more than that. It's not a lack of discipline, it's a lack of dopamine. It's not a need for structure, it's a different architecture of the brain. Showing your loved one that you understand this and are willing to listen to their experiences and give them your support will help them to weather the storm of these common misperceptions. It's okay not to understand everything at once, the important thing is that you are trying, are willing to learn, and are approaching any potential symptoms nonjudgmentally. As you progress through your learning journey, don't be afraid to ask questions, read books, go down a research wormhole on Google. There is also a plethora of support groups out there for the friends and family members of people with ADHD that can be a valuable source of anecdotal information on what might be helpful. No matter what avenue you choose, the key thing is to listen and learn. Your loved one will thank you for it.

CHAPTER 5
Pinpointing Your Strengths

So much of the way that we talk about ADHD focuses on the negatives. The DSM-5 criteria for diagnosis use terms like "fails," "avoids," and "difficulty." Even the title of the whole condition uses the word "deficit," for goodness' sake! With all of this linguistic doom and gloom, it's no wonder why so many people with ADHD struggle with their self-esteem. With this constant use of disparaging language, how can one possibly wade through and build their own confidence? We tend to forget that ADHD can also endow us with strengths, and while these certainly vary from person to person, we can follow some common themes to discover our individual assets and put them to use.

Building your life and your environment around your strengths will prevent you from feeling the constant need to mask your symptoms and will enable you to take the time to rest when you need to. Instead of constantly forcing yourself to meet neurotypical norms—and stumbling into the inevitable pitfalls of this plan—you can find ways to express your neurodivergence without fear of having accusations of being "weird" thrown at you. You probably *are* weird! Weird and wonderful! It's time to embrace that unflinchingly and make your weirdness work for you. This can be done in many ways, and through many career paths, based on your own personal strengths—which we will explore later in this chapter—but there are some commonalities in how the ADHD brain works that may give you some ideas before we knuckle down to this individual assessment of skills.

People with ADHD tend to be remarkably creative. Executive dysfunction—specifically that related to attention control—makes you a lateral thinker. Those odd, seemingly off-topic questions and remarks that you sometimes make are an expression of that ability to think outside the box. Being easily distracted—through the cognitive flexibility and inhibition elements of executive dysfunction—also contributes to the way that many people with ADHD are capable of thinking about things in a way that neurotypicals often don't allow their minds to pursue. For this very reason, it's thought that Leonardo Da Vinci, Pablo Picasso, and Albert Einstein all had ADHD, and this allowed for the creativity that is now lauded as "genius." Celebrated comedians Howie Mandel, Russell Brand, and Hannah Gadsby have all used their neurodivergence to produce humorous takes on situations that no neurotypical comedian had ever considered. Actresses Emma Watson and Zooey Deschanel have channeled their ADHD into creating moving and uplifting performances in TV and film. Acting, singing, playing an instrument, painting, drawing, sewing, writing, engineering, architecture, product development, industrial design, and coding are all ways to unleash your inner creativity, and they are just the tip of the iceberg. Whatever your interests are, there are ways of introducing a creative element to almost anything.

Similarly, the cognitive flexibility and cognitive inhibition elements involved in executive dysfunction also mean that people with ADHD are excellent at thinking on their feet and are more capable of seeing the bigger picture of a situation than many neurotypical people. Individuals with ADHD are great at out-of-the-box thinking and are often extraordinarily perceptive. I remember a time not too long ago when my sister, who normally doesn't even notice when I get my hair cut, realized that I was coming down with tonsillitis a full 24 hours before I was willing to believe her, all based on a minor change in the tonal range of my voice that she had previously noticed when I was sick. This intuitive sensory perception makes people with ADHD great leaders as they can manage teams effectively and empathize and collaborate with team members without resorting to micromanagement. This is also why ADHD is present in so many successful athletes, such as Shaquille O'Neal and Terry Bradshaw. These quick-thinking skills make for a team player who can make advantageous split-second decisions during a game. In the case of the hyperactive/impulsive ADHD subtype, excess energy can even translate to increased stamina in sport; another upper hand granted to athletes with the condition. This also shows that the strengths of ADHD can even be broken down according to the various subtypes.

People with the inattentive presentation of the condition care deeply about the things that they do focus on. They can be especially emotionally intelligent, remarkably insightful, and empathetic. This subtype also allows people to be remarkably adaptive, and individuals with the inattentive presentation of ADHD cope with transitional periods much more fluidly than do the other subtypes. They handle change, chaos, and confusion significantly more easily than the average person, and for this reason can be very successful in high-pressure career paths such as being paramedics, firefighters, personal assistants, and chefs.

In the impulsive/hyperactive form of ADHD, the inhibitory control element of executive dysfunction allows individuals to be adventurous risk-takers, and this translates to a common drive towards entrepreneurship. While you might struggle in the confines of overly-structured educational institutions and regimented workplaces, becoming an entrepreneur allows you much more flexibility. This career choice also removes the inertia that so often follows being told to do something by an authority figure. By creating a business that you are wholeheartedly interested in, your "hyperactivity" can even be harnessed, and hyper focusing on that topic will be beneficial.

Even outside of self-employment, this drive for adventure that is so often present in the impulsive/hyperactive presentation of ADHD can be a real strength. The need for dopamine and adrenaline allows people with ADHD to focus on multiple tasks far better than their neurotypical peers. This multitasking allows for a continual sense of productivity and achievement, which boosts dopamine usage and resultantly increases motivation to continue to take on more tasks. This thirst for continuous short tasks, and the ability to do multiple things at once, makes for incredibly talented nurses, childcare workers, stage managers, construction workers, and bartenders.

In the combined subtype of ADHD, individuals are commonly great conversationalists. The inattentive elements give them that out-of-the-box thinking, and the impulsive/hyperactive element leads to a reduction in inhibition and social anxiety in most cases. This means that people with the combined presentation of the condition tend to be engaging, witty speakers, who know how to command attention in a crowded room. They can spark intriguing lines of discussion without overthinking a situation in the way that a neurotypical person might, and this makes them great public speakers, trial lawyers, teachers, and television journalists.

Furthermore, one way of looking at the many misconceptions of ADHD is to see it as a silver lining that people with the condition are very often resilient; they have no choice but to be when the world is working against their neurotype. If you're constantly having to face the adversities placed in your path by a neurotypical society, you learn to eventually build up a thick skin and, once you have that, you might as well make use of it. Overcoming these sorts of obstacles and challenges means that people with ADHD tend to bounce back in the face of newly encountered hardships much more quickly than neurotypical people who haven't spent their entire lives being chastised for simply existing with a different neurotype. It sucks that the structure of society has meant that you have had plenty of practice picking yourself up after being knocked down, but you can make the best of a bad lot by using this resilience to your advantage. This forced resilience can contribute to having skills with troubleshooting various problems, as you are used to persevering until you find a system that works, and this problem-solving talent will serve you well in any walk of life.

In many people, these repeated adversities also inspire a strong sense of justice and fairness. As a result, many ADHD individuals stumble into roles of advocacy for others. After having themselves faced battling for acceptance, respect, a diagnosis, and accommodations, many people with ADHD become aware of the myriad of other ways that people are marginalized by the current structure of capitalist society. This realization often prompts a strong desire to speak out in favor of change, and here too the inhibitory control aspect of executive dysfunction becomes a strength, as you are not afraid to speak your mind. Cognitive flexibility also makes people with ADHD powerful debaters, adjusting to every counterargument, bobbing and weaving their line of reasoning like the Muhammad Ali of activism.

While some of these strengths may sound familiar to you, you may have completely discounted others as you read through the beginning of this chapter. As humans, we all tend to underestimate our assets and overestimate our perceived flaws. For that reason, it is useful to have access to a more formal technique to discover our true skills. Below, I have included adapted extracts from the *Executive Skills Questionnaire for Adults* to aid you in this self-assessment (Dawson & Guare, 2010).

Please keep in mind that this is an executive functioning questionnaire and, as such, anyone with ADHD will need to disagree with a large amount of the statements included. That's okay. We're simply looking for the ones that you disagree with the least or agree with the most. While these questions might feel like a harsh indictment of your condition, they are actually an opportunity to embrace your true self. It's okay to disagree with many of the statements. You are different, not wrong. This isn't a test, and there are no incorrect answers. No one but you ever need to see what you have answered, so try to be honest and acknowledge your strengths and challenges open-mindedly. This isn't a professional diagnosis, but rather a tool used by clinicians that we as laypeople can also benefit from using. The information provided to us will help in the next step toward building a life that works with your ADHD.

Executive Skills Questionnaire for Adults

"Looking at How We Plan, Manage Our Time and Respond to Stressors"
(Adapted from Peg Dawson & Richard Guare)

Instructions:

1. Read each item and then rate that item based on the extent to which you agree or disagree with how well it describes you. Use the rating scale below to choose the appropriate score. Be as honest as possible—the more honest you are, the more accurate the results will be.

Strongly disagree	= 1
Disagree	= 2
Tend to disagree	= 3
Neutral	= 4
Tend to agree	= 5
Agree	= 6
Strongly agree	= 7

2. As you answer all the items, make note of your score for each item.

3. Add the scores for each section, with each section including three items. The three highest sectional scores will show your executive skill strengths, according to the scoring key located below the items.

Items:

	Score:	Section Total:
1. I don't jump to conclusions. 2. I think before I speak. 3. I don't take action without having all the facts	1. 2. 3.	Section Total:
4. I have a good memory for facts, dates, and details 5. I am very good at remembering the things I have committed to do. 6. I seldom need reminders to complete tasks	Score: 4. 5. 6.	Section Total:
7. My emotions seldom get in the way when performing on the job. 8. Little things do not affect me emotionally or distract me from the task at hand. 9. I can defer my personal feelings until after a task has been completed.	Score: 7. 8. 9.	Section Total:
10. No matter what the task, I believe in getting started as soon as possible. 11. Procrastination is usually not a problem for me. 12. I seldom leave tasks to the last minute	Score: 10. 11. 12.	Section Total:
13. I find it easy to stay focused on my work 14. Once I start an assignment, I work diligently until it's completed. 15. Even when interrupted, I find it easy to get back and complete the job at hand.	Score: 13. 14. 15.	Section Total:
16. When I plan out my day, I identify priorities and stick to them 17. When I have a lot to do, I can easily focus on the most important things. 18. I typically break big tasks down into subtasks and timelines.	Score: 16. 17. 18.	Section Total:
19. I am an organized person. 20. It is natural for me to keep my work area neat and organized. 21. I am good at maintaining systems for organizing my work.	Score: 19. 20. 21.	Section Total:

22. At the end of the day, I've usually finished what I set out to do. 23. I am good at estimating how long it takes to do something. 24. I am usually on time for appointments &activities.	Score: 22. 23. 24.	Section Total:
25. I take unexpected events in stride. 26. I easily adjust to changes in plans and priorities. 27. I consider myself to be flexible and adaptive to change.	Score: 25. 26. 27.	Section Total:
28. I routinely evaluate my performance and devise methods for personal improvement. 29. I am able to step back from a situation in order to make objective decisions. 30. I "read" situations well and can adjust my behavior based on the reactions of others.	Score: 28. 29. 30.	Section Total:
31. I think of myself as being driven to meet my goals. 32. I easily give up immediate pleasures to work on long-term goals. 33. I believe in setting and achieving high levels of performance.	Score: 31. 32. 33.	Section Total:
34. I enjoy working in a highly demanding, fast-paced environment. 35. A certain amount of pressure helps me to perform at my best. 36. Jobs that include a fair degree of unpredictability appeal to me.	Score: 34. 35. 36.	Section Total:

Scoring:

Items	Executive Skill
1–3	Response Inhibition
4–6	Working Memory
7–9	Emotional Control
10–12	Task Initiation
13–15	Sustained Attention
16–18	Planning/Prioritization
19–21	Organization
22–24	Time Management
25–27	Flexibility
28–30	Metacognition
31–33	Goal-Directed Persistence
34–36	Stress Tolerance

What These Mean:
Dawson & Guare (2010) include the following definitions of these executive skills, which are used by clinicians and patients around the globe to determine areas of focus for the treatment of various challenges and the utilization of an individual's executive skill strengths.

Response Inhibition: The capacity to think before you act—this ability to resist the urge to say or do something allows us the time to evaluate a situation and how our behavior might impact it.

Working Memory: The ability to hold information in memory while performing complex tasks. It incorporates the ability to draw on past learning or experience to apply to the situation at hand or to project into the future.

Emotional Control: The ability to manage emotions in order to achieve goals, complete tasks, or control and direct behavior.

Sustained Attention: The capacity to maintain attention to a situation or task despite distractibility, fatigue, or boredom.

Task Initiation: The ability to begin projects without undue procrastination, in an efficient or timely fashion.

Planning/Prioritization: The ability to create a roadmap to reach a goal or to complete a task. It also involves being able to make decisions about what's important to focus on and what's not important.

Organization: The ability to create and maintain systems to keep track of information or materials.

Time Management: The capacity to estimate how much time one has, how to allocate it, and how to stay within time limits and deadlines. It also involves a sense that time is important.

Goal-Directed Persistence: The capacity to have a goal, follow through to the completion of the goal, and not be put off by or distracted by competing interests.

Flexibility: The ability to revise plans in the face of obstacles, setbacks, new information, or mistakes. It relates to adaptability to changing conditions.

Metacognition: The ability to stand back and take a birds-eye view of oneself in a situation. It is an ability to observe how you problem-solve. It also includes self-monitoring and self-evaluative skills (e.g., asking yourself, "How am I doing?" or "How did I do?" or "How did what I did affect other people?").

Stress Tolerance: The ability to thrive in stressful situations and to cope with uncertainty, change, and performance demands.

From this knowledge of your own strengths and challenges within your executive skill set, you can go on to create your diagnosis action plan.

Th is will be a goal-oriented plan of how you would like to adjust your environment to favor a given executive skill strength or accommodate your executive dysfunction challenges—which are signifi ed by the lowest three sectional scores of the questionnaire above. It is crucial that you keep your aims realistic and remember, again, to work *with* your ADHD rather than against it. Th is action plan is not intended to be an opportunity to beat yourself up and shame yourself into meeting neurotypical norms. Th is is a chance to decide how you want to adjust your life to meet your needs.

 BRAIN BREAK:

In ancient Athens, only the top 1% of wealth-holders paid taxes. Reaching the taxable wealth bracket was seen as a source of pride and was something they would often brag about. Contributing to the good of the community was seen as the ultimate expression of "usefulness" and the wealthy would often petition to pay more than their required share of taxes, just to prove that they could (Fouriezos, 2020).

Your diagnosis action plan is a means to evaluating where you're at with managing your ADHD, deciding on goals, and figuring out how to achieve them. You can have more than one of these plans at once or work on one goal at a time creating new plans as you go. Your diagnosis action plan can also address as narrow or as broad a situation as you see fit. This is about you finding out what works for you. No plan will ever be exactly what you need, but the goal is to become more and more aware of your strengths and challenges, and to be capable of evaluating what changes are needed to work with them. For that reason, I must stress that it's *completely* okay if you find yourself straying from the goals that you set yourself now. The key aspect here is to get something on paper. This will be your fallback. When you find yourself frustrated by how your executive dysfunction is presenting itself in a given area of your life, you can check back with your plan to recognize how your environment has continued to exacerbate your symptoms or been a barrier to your progress, and what steps you can take to rectify this. No one expects you to be perfect. Progress means far more than perfection. Allow yourself to take the first step towards progress by making this plan.

Your Diagnosis Action Plan

Step 1: Establish your goal

What executive skill is involved?

....

What will a successful intervention achieve?

....

Step 2: Decide what environmental support is needed

What barriers are currently in my environment? (e.g., distractions, lack of stimuli, social complexities, etc.) What can I do to change these?

....

What barriers exist within this specific circumstance? (e.g., long timespan, no breaks, no reward for completion) What can I do to change these?

....

What external support from another person might be useful? (e.g., body doubling, praise, reminders)

....

....

Step 3: Determine a procedure to enact as many of these changes as possible (e.g., setting timers for breaks, asking a friend to body double, using background music, etc.)

....

....

Step 4: Plan for the future

What incentives can I use to ensure that I continue to safeguard myself from similar barriers? (e.g., praise, something to look forward to, a menu of rewards to choose from, etc. Plan for daily, weekly, and long-term incentives)

....

....

What skills can I learn, practice, and use to continue my progress?

....

Step 5: Know how to measure success

How will I measure my outcome and know that my intervention was successful?

....

Plans such as this can be made and used as often or as rarely as you like; they are simply an opportunity for self-awareness and accountability. As mentioned previously, you won't always stick to the original details of the plan. That's okay. Despite that, and because of that, try to continue to persevere with making the plans anyway. Each time that you encourage your mind to think about how you can work with your condition, and every opportunity you take to remind yourself that you are allowed to make changes and ask for help, will strengthen those neural pathways and make it easier for you to think in that way in the future. The nature of ADHD means that no method or technique will ever be a permanent fixture in your life, and that's alright. Your brain needs variety, and so these plans will only be a temporary measure. While they are new to you, engage with them wholeheartedly and truly take the time to reflect, but don't force yourself to stick with something that isn't working for you. Tailor these methods to your own needs, and when they aren't doing the trick any longer, find new accessible techniques to replace them with.

Also, don't forget to give yourself a pat on the back. This much introspection can be uncomfortable. I wholeheartedly acknowledge that. The fact that you are willing to engage with this process in order to improve your quality of life is a huge credit to you and you deserve praise for that. Whoever came up with the nonsense phrase, "Self-praise is no praise," clearly had plenty of dopamine and got a bit cocky about it. Self-praise is an incredibly useful tool in encouraging yourself to stick with boring or uncomfortable new ways of thinking. I know that when you aren't used to this kind of thinking, praising yourself can feel incredibly egotistical. This is especially true when you have spent a large portion of your life being berated as lazy or unproductive. But, allow me to reassure you, your discomfort is from experiencing something new, not from doing something wrong. You are allowed to be proud of yourself. You *should* be proud of yourself. You are also allowed to be compassionate towards yourself if you find that your inner criticism shouts particularly loudly when you try to feel proud of yourself. Expressing compassion and satisfaction with yourself isn't arrogance; it's kindness, and you deserve that.

CHAPTER 6
Protecting Your Progress
for Success

It is vitally important to be kind to yourself, not only for the sake of your own mental health and emotional well-being, but to protect the advances you have made in self-acceptance and self-compassion as you have worked through this book. Though positivity will never help you to manifest your way to perfect mental health, taking a positive mindset on your ADHD and your ability to manage it will safeguard the progress you make in learning to manage your condition. This is because there are several extremely common negative tendencies, such as harsh critiquing self-talk, which have the potential to hinder your progress. In this chapter, we will work on awareness and avoidance of these bad habits, as well as additional methods of preserving your progress going forward.

Each of us has, inside our minds, that inner critic that judges our actions and regularly demeans us for them. In moderation, this can sometimes be a motivator for change. However, far more regularly, this critical inner voice makes us question our self-worth and undermines our confidence in ourselves. The inner critic regularly parrots the criticisms that you have heard most often externally, without ever allowing you the opportunity to logically evaluate whether such criticisms are a valid reflection of your behavior. The critic levels these aspersions at you to attempt to prompt a behavioral change which would prevent you from hearing those criticisms from anyone else ever again, but a behavioral change is not always necessary, or even possible; and where it is possible, the behavior that your inner critic attempts to prompt may not be in line with your personal belief system.

For people with ADHD, the commonly cast insults are that you are "lazy," "bone-idle," "a chronic procrastinator," "unmotivated," "stupid," "a ditz," "a clutz," or any one of an abundance of negative misconceptions surrounding executive dysfunction. Consequently, these are the exact phrases that your inner critic is most likely to attack you with when you need rest. But those insults are not a reflection of who you are. You haven't been any of those things, and even if you had been, everyone is lazy and unmotivated from time to time; that doesn't mean that we are worthless or useless. You are neurodivergent. You have executive dysfunction. While you can learn techniques to manage and work around that to some degree, the executive dysfunction itself is not, and won't ever be, within your control—barring some completely unprecedented leap in neuroscientific research, and even if that did occur, is neurodiversity something we really should be aiming to "cure?" I think not.

Some of us have been around long enough to remember when children used to be beaten for writing with their left hand. The hand would be tied behind their back until they learned to write "normally", and this "intervention" was seen as par for the course at the time. Yet now, we look back in horror, realizing the abuse that was so needlessly inflicted on young children to "correct" something that was never actually a flaw to begin with. This is tantamount to the harm that you inflict upon yourself by attempting to bully yourself into acting neurotypical. It doesn't work like that. Research shows that converted former left-handers have additional strain in the sensorimotor cortex of their brains even after decades of writing with their right hand (Siebner et al., 2002). So, how much harm is your self-criticism doing by attempting to change far more of your behavior than just your handwriting?

Remaining up-to-date in your self-education about ADHD and its impacts can help to waylay this harsh self-talk, as you will have the facts with which to refute it, just as you would refute an obstinately bigoted family member or friend. Hearing about other people's experiences with similar struggles can help you to recognize that, while your ADHD is an inseparable part of you, it is not *all* of you, and therefore, your symptoms are not you, they are your condition. Separating yourself from the behaviors that your inner critic latches onto in this way can help to create the mental headspace with which to challenge that criticism. Your symptoms are not a representation of your character. Read that again: Your symptoms are <u>not</u> a representation of your character.

Positive mantras—such as the sentence above—are an excellent tool for challenging your inner critic. By having a few go-to responses for your most common self-criticisms, you can fight them without becoming overwhelmed by the need to construct an argument in the moment. These can include general statements used to reaffirm your self-worth or specific counterarguments against common criticisms, and while I understand that such affirmations can sometimes feel silly, they are once again building up those neural pathways that will help you escape this inner negativity. I have included examples of possible mantras below, but I encourage you to create two or three of your own as well. Creating an easily accessible list of these mantras will help you to engage with them.

One such option is to stick them to the door or your refrigerator, or your bathroom mirror, but both my sister and I have found that these options too easily become background information that is ignored within a day or two. Creating a list in the notes app of your smartphone, screenshotting it, and setting it as your lock and home screen backgrounds can be an excellent option. This is something that most people will look at over 50 times each day and will cause you to read and internalize these mantras even without meaning to. A further option that is incredibly effective, though not comfortable to everyone, is recording yourself or a loved one saying these mantras and setting that voice note as the sound for your morning alarm. Our semi-conscious brains are far more receptive to positivity than our fully-conscious selves, and this can be an easy way to ensure that you engage with the mantras on a regular basis. Of course, these are merely suggestions, and I highly encourage you to implement whatever system you think will be most accessible to you. Some example mantras include:

- My symptoms are not a representation of my character.
- I am doing the best that I can.
- I deserve to respect my limitations.
- Progress is better than perfection.
- I am allowed to spend energy on myself.
- Resting is not the same as being lazy.
- I am allowed to rest.
- Productivity is not synonymous with worth.
- I am worthy.
- It's okay to put my needs first.
- Setting boundaries is healthy.
- I am loveable, just as I am.
- I am allowed to ask for help.
- Done is better than perfect.
- I will meet myself where I'm at.
- The only person I need to keep up with is myself.

These kinds of simple sentences are a worthwhile way to remind yourself of some basic truths that are too easily swept aside by misconceptions of ADHD. Keeping them near to hand will empower you to access that inner truth and reject the stigma surrounding the condition. This, in turn, will help remind you to play to your strengths and not get caught up in your challenges.

As mentioned in the previous chapter, people with ADHD—obviously—each have their own individual strengths, but some of the more common advantageous traits of the condition can be cultivated in everyone, and this will bolster your progress as you move forward into self-acceptance. You are most likely energetic, innovative, and spontaneous, and each of these characteristics makes you who you are. They can be harnessed and directed towards the things that interest you—enabling you to hyper focus, guilt-free—to help you rather than act as the hindrance you may have so often been told that they would be.

Likewise, while the depression of dopamine levels in your brain can quite often act to create inertia, it can also be utilized in your favor. A 2017 study made by psychologists at the University of Amsterdam and published in the *Journal of Attention Disorders* showed that, when motivated through competition or rewards, adults with ADHD experienced "enhanced real-world creative achievements" (Boot et al., 2017). Importantly, these researchers also found that there was no impediment to creativity in the adults who were taking pharmaceutical medications for their ADHD. You are capable of seeing the world's weirdness and putting it to good use; you just need to have a little faith in your own capabilities.

A fundamental instrument in this self-empowerment is, of course, your support system. As detailed in Chapter 4, the value of your support network mustn't be underestimated. Friendships protect our mental health and build our sense of self-worth, so it is vital that we cherish and maintain these grounding influences. In addition to being our source of a sense of belonging, a shoulder to cry on, and a cheerleader through our triumphs, our friends are also a powerful source of motivation that can enhance dopamine production in the brains of ADHDers. One key element of ADHD coaching is the use of targeted praise as a focused dopamine inducer to prompt inner motivation. But you don't need a professionally trained coach for that; your loved ones can just as easily help you with this neural training, and that is part of the importance of supportive and like-minded friendships. In 2015, researchers found that although students in third-level education were rarely aware of the academic achievements of their peers, they tended to unconsciously mirror them regardless of their own previously attained grades (Dokuka et al., 2015). Likewise, our friends impact our achievements in our careers. Studies have shown that individuals who experience loneliness in their private lives are 62% more likely to be perceived by their colleagues as being unapproachable, whereas people who feel secure in their friendship groups reach significantly higher levels of employee performance (Ozcelik & Barsade, 2011).

Specific to ADHD, supportive socializing appears to be more significantly beneficial to one's symptoms than even medication (Haverkampf, 2016). For this reason, it has even been suggested that the development of healthy friendships be considered a form of treatment for ADHD (Mikami, 2010). So, how do we go about cultivating this form of support?

Many people who struggle with their mental health or neurotype often feel ashamed to admit that they need the support of their friends. We fear being perceived as a burden, and we worry that the balance of our friendships will be altered by any additional vulnerability. But friendships are meant to be built on mutual support. You shouldn't have to feel as though you need to "earn" the care and attention of your loved ones. Though it may feel tough, it is important that we learn to lean on our friends in times of need. Humans are social creatures for a reason, and we are designed to both need and provide this kind of support. This kind of reciprocal giving and receiving of social support is so vital to human health that a study at the Department of Psychological and Brain Sciences at Johns Hopkins University in 2006 showed that it reduces our risk of high blood pressure and associated heart disease (Piferi & Lawler, 2006). Telling your loved ones about your experiences with ADHD can not only provide you with support but will also help to improve their understanding of your strengths and challenges.

If your friend or family member hasn't been privy to your diagnostic process, seeking this kind of support and understanding comes with a process not unlike coming out about one's sexuality. You may need to decide on an appropriate time and method of telling them about your condition and explaining the ways in which it affects you. It can be useful to choose a time and place that is comfortable for both of you, as this will immediately lead to less tension and anxiety. If you would be more comfortable discussing this via phone or text, where you can take an extra moment to think before responding, then do that. Take whatever path feels most comfortable to you. It's your diagnosis, and it's your decision how and when to disclose it. Practicing vocalizing a few key elements that you want to communicate can help you to get the information across smoothly, but it is also okay to play it by ear and decide on your phraseology as you observe how your friend or family member is responding.

Keep in mind that most people won't have encountered a situation or disclosure like this before and, as a result, they may react differently than you had hoped. A lot of neurotypicals feel awkward and at a loss for words when someone reveals that they are neurodivergent. Remind yourself that they simply need time to process the news, and that their silence isn't a condemnation. It can be helpful to have the names of a few reliable sources of information on hand to refer them to if they respond unfavorably. Just remember, if they truly care about you, they will want you to be comfortable expressing your true self. If they continuously put you under pressure to mask your symptoms— telling you to "just pull yourself together"—it may be time to move on from the relationship.

At the end of the day, protecting your progress translates to protecting yourself, and this involves taking responsibility when your relationships are proving detrimental. Hopefully, as an adult, you have the power to walk away from anyone who is harming your emotional well-being. Where the relationship is of deep importance to you, it can be worth pushing through trying to educate the person. But even in the case of a person you have known your entire life, it's okay to decide that you need your mental health more than them. It is better to adjust your lifestyle to their absence than to change your boundaries to accommodate continued disrespect.

Thankfully, these situations are rare. In most cases, your friends and loved ones may need a little time to come to terms with the new information, but will then be willing to understand, respect, and support you through managing your ADHD. So, don't be afraid to lean on them when you need to. Asking a loved one to sit with you while you work through a task may seem like a big deal to you but, nine times out of ten, they won't mind in the slightest. Feel free to discuss with your friends and family what supports they are and aren't comfortable providing, so that you know who to ask in various situations. Some family members may feel comfortable sourcing information about treatment services but may prefer not to attend appointments with you. Some friends may be more than happy to sit with you while you cook but hate the smell of cleaning products. If you have a friend that is training to be an accountant, they may be delighted to help you manage your finances, whereas an English Literature graduate may be more comfortable helping you to respond to emails.

Be upfront about the kinds of help you may need and keep notes on who is willing to help and in what ways. If you have quite a small inner circle, you may all be in the habit of providing each other with a lot of support anyway. If you tend to flit between various social groups, it may be helpful to keep tabs on who you have asked for help recently to avoid overwhelming any one friend or friend group. There are a multitude of apps that can help you to formally keep track of this sort of thing, but often I find that it's easy to forget that you have even downloaded these apps. It tends to be more helpful in the long run to attempt to build the habit of taking a moment to check in with yourself before asking for help. This split second of self-awareness can be an opportunity to reassure yourself that it's okay to ask for help, as well as a chance to evaluate who you should turn to for this assistance. Protecting your progress also involves protecting your support network, so make sure that your loved ones know that it's okay to say no to you. They have their own challenges to cope with and will need to gain an understanding of their own limits and ability to set boundaries. In fact, for people with ADHD, hearing "no" in the cases of smaller requests for assistance can help to strengthen your inner stability from the rejection-sensitive dysphoria that so often creeps into our minds in the case of larger denials or refusals. This inner fortitude will enable you to take appropriate risks and excel in the fields of life that mean the most to you.

BRAIN BREAK:

One of the branded Original Parts created by the Volkswagen car company is a sausage!

You read that correctly, the car manufacturer also makes a sausage; a hot dog; a wiener; or to be more precise, a currywurst. Because of the remote whereabouts of their production factories, Volkswagen has had an onsite canteen since 1938. In 1974, their original curried sausage was born, and in the years since it has gone on to win a variety of awards. In fact, the VW currywurst has been so successful that, with a production run of 6.8 million units in 2018, Volkswagen actually makes more sausages than cars! They have even expanded to making their own ketchup and cutlery to accompany the currywurst ("Why does Volkswagen make sausages? Reasons Behind the Currywurst", 2020).

No singular technique will ever enable you to "overcome" your condition—and indeed, this is not the goal you should be working towards—but by overlapping a multitude of skills and supports, you can maintain your sense of mastery over your life and feel that you have ADHD; not that ADHD has you. Remember that not every difficulty that you encounter is as a result of your condition, and that even the most emotionally-stable neurotypicals have an occasional meltdown. It's okay to need support. It's not a weakness to need help. You have the skills at hand to live the life you want to lead; the most difficult step is remembering that fact.

One such skill is knowing how to effectively ask for help using an appropriate level of assertion without coming across as aggressive. Marsha Linehan, who developed Dialectical Behavior Therapy with the goal of helping her patients regulate their emotions, dedicates a section of her book *DBT Skills Training Handouts and Worksheets* to this very issue. She includes a list of ten questions to help individuals evaluate how assertively to make a specific request, which I have adapted below with ADHD needs in mind:

1. Is this person capable of giving or doing what I want?
2. In this situation, is getting this form of support more important than potentially damaging our relationship or my view of myself? (How do I want to prioritize my needs, my relationship with this person, and my self-respect?)
3. Will the support that I'm requesting help me feel competent and capable?
4. Is the person required by law or moral code to do or give me what I want?
5. Do I have the authority to tell this person what to do?
6. Is my request appropriate to the type of relationship I have with this person?
7. In the long-term, would I regret not receiving the support that I'm asking for?

8. Do I make sure to reciprocate with mutual support for this person? (Do I give roughly as much as I get?)
9. Do I know exactly what I want and have the facts I need to support my request? (Am I capable of clearly communicating my exact request and receiving informed consent from the other person?)
10. Is now a good time to ask? (Am I sure that the other person is not hungry, tired, under the influence of drugs or alcohol, or in any situation that might alter their decision-making skills?)

For each question that you answer yes to, it is appropriate to increase the intensity of the way that you request the support. If you find yourself answering no to every single question, you shouldn't ask for or even hint at your support needs with this person. With three to six yeses, you can openly make a gentle request, but be willing to accept a rejection immediately. With seven or eight yeses, there is room for negotiation and it's appropriate to stand your ground and firmly request support. When this number approaches ten, you can insist that your request is met without doubting yourself for not taking no for an answer. As the people around you become more and more familiar with your support needs, this process should become easier and easier.

People with ADHD tend to be fueled by their passions, and self-care can become your passion. You can protect your progress using those very same aspects of ADHD that once required you to make that progress in the first place. Where once your ADHD-fed intensity was channeled into your inner critic, you can redirect that same intensity to your love of self-acceptance and your need to self-advocate. I don't mean to imply that any of this is easy—the sustained effort of changing one's train of thought repeatedly is no small task —but it is possible, and you have the ability to enact this change. Trust me, it will be worth it.

This is another aspect in which a counselor or, more specifically, an ADHD coach can be of huge benefit. These professionals can encourage you to embrace your ADHD as a tool for change and success. Your energy, impulsivity, intuition, creativity, ability to multitask, hyper focus, and intelligence can all become part of the toolbox that you use to work towards your version of a fulfilling life, and an ADHD coach can guide you through this process nonjudgmentally and at your own pace. ADHD can and has been a major factor in the success of many businesspeople, athletes, and performers, and it can help you to reach the apex version of yourself as well.

For instance, British chef Jamie Oliver was diagnosed with ADHD and dyslexia as a child and has gone on to use his intense passions and creativity to devise healthy flavor-packed recipes, as well as advocating for the understanding and support of children with learning disabilities. Likewise, Erin Brockovich-Ellis—the face of America's largest class-action lawsuit and the subject of the award-winning 2000 film starring Julia Roberts—initially struggled academically and was told by teachers that she wouldn't make it through college, yet went on to become a legal clerk and activist who would be instrumental in building the winning case against the Pacific Gas & Electric Company of California in 1993.

Prior to being diagnosed and treated for ADHD, Major League Baseball's Scott Eyre could hardly focus on or remember conversations with his loved ones and teammates. After having his executive dysfunction issues noticed by his team's therapist, Time Hewes, Eyre went on to be diagnosed with ADHD as an adult in 2001. He has been very vocal about the difference that this process has made to his life saying, "I think that my ADHD was something that I drew strength from due to all the energy I had. As a relief pitcher, I felt like I could pitch every day" (Eyre & Grünke, 2020). Eyre's acceptance of his diagnosis empowered him to take the step to medication, and he has gone on to state, "If I had one wish, I'd wish I could go back to high school and take my medication every day. I could have accomplished so much more. But the more I learn now, the more I can get out to parents" (Eyre & Redfearn, 2019). You too can use your diagnosis and self-acceptance as a path to greatness.

Likewise, the very term "comorbid condition" sounds, well… morbid. But co-occurring diagnoses don't need to mean added suffering. For example, self-stimulating behavior—commonly referred to as stimming—is a frequently occurring symptom of autism. These repetitive movements, vocal patterns, and other behaviors include walking on tiptoes, hair twirling, hand flapping, the use of fidget toys, whistling, leg bouncing, and many others. These repetitions of movements or noises are a way for autistic people to regulate the over- or under-stimulation of their nervous systems, which helps them to avoid or manage burnouts and meltdowns. Importantly for the 61% of autistics who also have ADHD, it is thought that stimming revitalizes your dopamine receptors! So, the symptom of one condition becomes the treatment of another. Hair twirling, rocking back and forth, bouncing your leg, and so on become effective coping mechanisms for both ADHD and autism, through two different neurological processes, essentially helping you to manage both conditions.

Similarly, many people with anxiety disorders feel the need to plan for every possible eventuality. Using this nervous energy to build your support system and create a safety net for your struggles with executive dysfunction can be a way to channel a generally distressing condition into positive change. Again, that is of course easier said than done, but you do have the tools at your disposal to make the changes you want to see in your life. Just as with ADHD, any other diagnosis that you have can be worked with rather than struggled against. This practical application of self-acceptance is a vital element of protecting the progress that you make with your ADHD. If you accept only one part of yourself, instead of who you are as a whole, your inner critic is still left with far too much fuel for the fire of self-beratement.

Regardless of when, how, or if you were given your official ADHD diagnosis, you deserve to cherish your high energy, your risk-taking, your intuition, ability to multitask, out-of-the-box thinking, your hyper focus, any and all of the things that make you who you are; including your ADHD. Karina Smirnoff, of *Dancing with the Stars* fame, dealt with undiagnosed ADHD her entire life before getting an assessment well into her adulthood. But this didn't stop Smirnoff from finding ways to thrive with the condition, rather than simply survive through it. Her excess energy was channeled into her dancing career, and she has five world championship titles to show for it. The host of *Extreme Makeover: Home Edition*, Ty Pennington, has used his hyper focus and enthusiasm to work towards giving families in need dream-worthy housing, all after years of being berated by teachers and eventually dropping out of college.

You might not be built for the standard neurotypical goals like third-level education, but that is a problem with the inaccessibility of the system, not with you. These forms of systemic discrimination are incredibly difficult to deal with, but they don't mean that you can't have and reach your own goals. There is more than a single path towards any type of achievement. You are capable. You are competent. You are lovable, wonderful, and success-ready just as you are. If you aren't ready to believe in those statements, that is a product of our ableist society, not a representation of the truth. Your symptoms can be managed without being masked. Your condition can be reframed without being repressed. Your fight for focus can become a nirvana of neurodiversity. You are worth it.

CONCLUSION

The way that we think about ourselves and our role in the world plays a major part in our physical and mental health. Self-denial and inner criticism can damage your brain every bit as much as a stroke or a tumor. When I learned that, it struck me to my core. My pre-existing concern for my sister Renesmee, and the way that she viewed neurodiversity, grew exponentially as I came to terms with the long-term harms that this self-doubt could impose on her life. Being able to help her make her way through a journey of self-discovery and acceptance was the greatest gift I have ever received.

Everyone deserves to feel that they have a place in this world, but sadly that is so rarely the case for the neurodivergent. Society places such ableist expectations on our minds and bodies that any departure from these norms is pathologized and demonized. By reaching the conclusion of this book, you have already taken the first step towards shedding the shackles of those ridiculous "ideals," and you should be proud of yourself for that. In the modern age, we are so constantly bombarded with misinformation that it can be difficult to take a step back from the stigmas and stereotypes and embark on a journey of self-acceptance, but you have done that. For each person that rejects the misconceptions surrounding ADHD, we take another step towards a future where those stigmas no longer exist, and I thank you for being a part of that.

Though as individuals we, of course, don't have the power of multi-million dollar ad campaigns to change the views of the world—such as the National Dairy Council was able to do with milk, and BP Oil managed with recycling—each of us can still make a powerful impact in dismantling the stereotypes surrounding ADHD, and this process of unlearning begins within us.

You have seen the true nature of executive dysfunction. You have taken the time to understand some fundamental truths surrounding ADHD. You have equipped yourself with the knowledge that will enable you to collaborate with your neurodivergence rather than challenge it. But don't let this be the end of your journey. It's time to put that theory into practice. Keep learning, keep checking in with yourself, keep challenging flawed thinking about ADHD.

The science is there. More and more research about ADHD is being done every day. Challenge your healthcare providers to keep up-to-date with this information. Ask your loved ones to stay informed and continue learning. The true fight for focus isn't within the minds of people with ADHD; it's throughout the wider world—combatting the pigeonholing of ADHD as a disorder of misbehaved children. You deserve better. Every neurodivergent person deserves better than the way they are being spoken about, when you should be spoken with.

ADHD is not a diagnosis of doom. It's not a label of laziness or lack of motivation, and neurotypical people need to learn that. As they do, take care of yourself. Keep fighting the good fight, but also don't forget to practice self-care. You should not have to go through this battle alone. Surround yourself with a support network that truly understands, or at least is willing to admit when they don't, and learn more. Whether that involves formalized support groups or one close friend to call on is completely up to you but try not to neglect this part of your healing. Self-acceptance can only get you so far if it's not mirrored by external community care. This person or people will be your cheerleaders in times of triumph, your shoulder to cry on in challenging circumstances, and they will be another team member in the campaign to transform the way the world views and speaks about neurodiversity.

I have spent years researching this topic following Renesmee's diagnosis, and while I won't ask anyone to devote that same kind of time and energy to this learning journey, I truly hope that you and your loved ones will persevere for the sake of your physical, mental, and emotional well-being. There are so many ways that the desire to educate oneself can manifest and be utilized, and you are free to explore every option. Remember that the people living with the condition are the true experts, but also respect the science behind new information. Find reliable sources and means of spreading their information to others. Continue to challenge societal norms, even outside the scope of ADHD and neurodiversity. Let your own hardships be the path to understanding the marginalization of others. Take what you have learned about self-awareness and apply it to other aspects of your life. But most of all, be kind; to yourself and to others. Grant yourself and your loved ones some compassion as you stumble along this informative path together.

Life is hard already, and all the harder when you are facing the kinds of stigmatization that surround any divergence from white, CIS heteronormative, able-bodied, and neurotypical ideals. Try not to make it any more difficult by filling yourself with shame and blame when you find that you have slipped in your applications of the skills to manage your ADHD. If what you've been doing isn't working, that's a sign that it's time to move on and find something new. Executive (dys)function is fluid, and so too must our approach to handling it be. So, it's okay if you find yourself struggling against your symptoms even after you thought that you had learned to accept them. Keep coming back to this journey. Healing is cyclical, not linear, and if you have spent your entire life viewing your ADHD as a character flaw, of course it's going to take some time to learn to approach yourself and your symptoms in the spirit of collaboration. Don't be afraid to lean on your support network in these times. They can remind you of your strengths and help you protect the progress you have made. The ADHD affirmations in Chapter 6 can also remind you of some fundamental truths in these difficult times.

Not only are you capable of this self-acceptance and kindness, but you also deserve it. You don't need to earn the respect and love of people who truly care about you. You don't need to prove that you can be productive. You don't need to "overcome" or do anything "in spite of" your diagnosis. You can simply coexist with it. Take control of what you can and release everything else. Find what works for you. Live your life in your own spectacular, neurodivergent way. Again, as the saying goes, those who matter don't mind, and those who mind don't matter.

CONGRATULATIONS ON FINISHING!!!
I know it may have been hard for you to get this far, but give yourself a round of applause because you sure did it!

If you enjoyed the book and felt it added value to your life, please consider leaving an honest Amazon review of the book & feel free to share with others! Let's keep up the fight for focus and bringing awareness to ADHD!

★ ★ ★ ★ ★
amazon

Thank You!

REFERENCES

Ahmann, E., Saviett, M., & Tuttle, L. (2017). Emerging evidence for the effectiveness of coaching for attention deficit/hyperactivity disorder. In *Coaching in Leadership and Healthcare Conference*. Harvard Medical School.

All About Frogs. Burke Museum. (2021). Retrieved 6 August 2021, from https://www.burkemuseum.org/collections-and-research/biology/herpetology/all-about-amphibians/all-about-frogs.

All images sourced from unsplash.com

Ballentine, K. (2019). Understanding Racial Differences in Diagnosing ODD Versus ADHD Using Critical Race Theory. *Families In Society: The Journal of Contemporary Social Services*, *100*(3), 282-292. https://doi.org/10.1177/1044389419842765

Barkely, R. (2010). *Taking Charge of Adult ADHD*. The Guilford Press.

Barkley, R. (2018). *Attention-Deficit Hyperactivity Disorder: A Handbook for Diagnosis and Treatment* (4th ed.). Guilford Publications.

Biederman, J., Petty, C., Woodworth, K., Lomedico, A., Hyder, L., & Faraone, S. (2012). Adult Outcome of Attention-Deficit/Hyperactivity Disorder. *The Journal of Clinical Psychiatry*, *73*(07), 941-950. https://doi.org/10.4088/jcp.11m07529

Bloomfield, M., McCutcheon, R., Kempton, M., Freeman, T., & Howes, O. (2019). The effects of psychosocial stress on dopaminergic function and the acute stress response. *Elife*, 8. https://doi.org/10.7554/elife.46797

Boot, N., Nevicka, B., & Baas, M. (2017). Creativity in ADHD: Goal-Directed Motivation and Domain Specificity. *Journal Of Attention Disorders*, *24*(13), 1857-1866. https://doi.org/10.1177/1087054717727352

Bracken, H. (2021). *The Hunchback of Notre Dame*. Encyclopedia Britannica. https://www.britannica.com/topic/The-Hunchback-of-Notre-Dame.

Brown, T. (2013). *A new understanding of ADHD in children and adults: Executive function impairments*. Routledge.

Bukstein, O. (2007). Substance abuse in patients with attention-deficit/hyperactivity disorder. *Medscape Journal of Medicine*, *10*(1), 24.

Buss, D. (2005). *The handbook of evolutionary psychology*. Hoboken: Wiley & Sons.

Carlson, S., & Wang, T. (2007). Inhibitory control and emotion regulation in preschool children. *Cognitive Development*, *22*(4), 489-510. https://doi.org/10.1016/j.cogdev.2007.08.002

Cole, P., Weibel, S., Nicastro, R., Hastler, R., Dayer, A., & Aubry, J. et al. (2016). CBT/DBT skills training for adults with attention deficit hyperactivity disorder (ADHD). *Psychiatria Danubina*, *28*(1), 103-107.

Corbett, B., Constantine, L., Hendren, R., Rocke, D., & Ozonoff, S. (2009). Examining executive functioning in children with autism spectrum disorder, attention deficit hyperactivity disorder and typical development. *Psychiatry Research*, *166*(2-3), 210-222. https://doi.org/10.1016/j.psychres.2008.02.005

Corrigan, P. (2007). How Clinical Diagnosis Might Exacerbate the Stigma of Mental Illness. *Social Work*, *52*(1), 31-39. https://doi.org/10.1093/sw/52.1.31

Cox, J. (2019). *The Secret to My Success with ADD? A Support Network of One*. ADDitude. Retrieved 29 July 2021, from https://www.additudemag.com/support-network-adults-with-add/.

Dalsgaard, S., Østergaard, S., Leckman, J., Mortensen, P., & Pedersen, M. (2015). Mortality in children, adolescents, and adults with attention deficit hyperactivity disorder: a nationwide cohort study. *The Lancet*, *385*(9983), 2190-2196. https://doi.org/10.1016/s0140-6736(14)61684-6

Danielson, M., Bitsko, R., Ghandour, R., Holbrook, J., Kogan, M., & Blumberg, S. (2018). Prevalence of Parent-Reported ADHD Diagnosis and Associated Treatment Among U.S. Children and Adolescents, 2016. *Journal Of Clinical Child & Adolescent Psychology*, *47*(2), 199-212. https://doi.org/10.1080/15374416.2017.1417860

Dawson, P., & Guare, R. (2010). *Executive skills in children and adolescents* (2nd ed.). Guilford Publications.

Dietz, W., Baur, L., Hall, K., Puhl, R., Taveras, E., Uauy, R., & Kopelman, P. (2015). Management of obesity: improvement of health-care training and systems for prevention and care. *The Lancet*, *385*(9986), 2521-2533. https://doi.org/10.1016/s0140-6736(14)61748-7

Dokuka, S., Valeeva, D., & Yudkevich, M. (2015). The Diffusion of Academic Achievements: Social Selection and Influence in Student Networks. *SSRN Electronic Journal*. https://doi.org/10.2139/ssrn.2658031

Eisenberg, D., & Campbell, B. (2011). The Evolution of ADHD: Social context matters. *San Francisco Medicine*, *Oct*.

Eisenberg, D., Campbell, B., Gray, P., & Sorenson, M. (2008). Dopamine receptor genetic polymorphisms and body composition in undernourished pastoralists: An exploration of nutrition indices among nomadic and recently settled Ariaal men of northern Kenya. *BMC Evolutionary Biology, 8*(1), 173. https://doi.org/10.1186/1471-2148-8-173

Eyre, S., & Grünke, M. (2020). "The Most Important Things in Life Are Good Friends and a Good Bullpen": An Interview with Scott Eyre About Playing Major League Baseball With ADHD and How the Sport Can Help Struggling Students to Succeed. *Insights Into Learning Disabilities, 17*(2), 129-138.

Eyre, S., & Redfearn, S. (2019). *A Giant Accomplishment*. ADDitude. Retrieved 28 July 2021, from https://www.additudemag.com/a-giant-accomplishment/.

Fadus, M., Ginsburg, K., Sobowale, K., Halliday-Boykins, C., Bryant, B., Gray, K., & Squeglia, L. (2019). Unconscious Bias and the Diagnosis of Disruptive Behavior Disorders and ADHD in African American and Hispanic Youth. *Academic Psychiatry, 44*(1), 95-102. https://doi.org/10.1007/s40596-019-01127-6

Fouriezos, N. (2020). *How Ancient Athens Convinced Its Wealthiest to Love Paying Taxes*. OZY. Retrieved 23 July 2021, from https://www.ozy.com/fast-forward/how-ancient-athens-convinced-its-wealthiest-to-love-paying-taxes/409789/.

Friedrichs, B., Igl, W., Larsson, H., & Larsson, J. (2010). Coexisting Psychiatric Problems and Stressful Life Events in Adults with Symptoms of ADHD—A Large Swedish Population-Based Study of Twins. *Journal Of Attention Disorders, 16*(1), 13-22. doi: 10.1177/1087054710376909

Gerhand, S., & Saville, C. (2021). ADHD prevalence in the psychiatric population. *International Journal of Psychiatry In Clinical Practice*, 1-13. https://doi.org/10.1080/13651501.2021.1914663

Gillberg, C., Gillberg, I., Rasmussen, P., Kadesjo, B., Soderstrom, H., & Rastam, M. et al. (2004). Coexisting disorders in ADHD: implications for diagnosis and intervention. *European Child & Adolescent Psychiatry*, *13*(S1). https://doi.org/10.1007/s00787-004-1008-4

Gorfein, D., & MacLeod, C. (2007). *Inhibition in cognition*. American Psychological Association.

Graye, S. (2018). *Accepting My ADHD Diagnosis Was a Lesson In Ableism*. HuffPost UK. Retrieved 28 July 2021, from https://www. huffingtonpost.co.uk/entry/accepting-my-adhd-diagnosis-a-personal-lesson-in-ableism_uk_5b16c948e4b099fa52f3ed9f.

Hallowell, E., & Dodson, W. (2018). *From Shame and Stigma to Pride and Truth: It's Time to Celebrate ADHD Differences*. Presentation, ADDitude Webinar.

Harper, D. (2021). **ghrei- | Origin and meaning of root *ghrei- by Online Etymology Dictionary*. Etymonline.com. Retrieved 1 August 2021, from https://www.etymonline.com/word/*ghrei-.

Harvard School of Public Health. (2017). *Poll finds at least half of Black Americans say they have experienced racial discrimination in their jobs and from the police*.

Haverkampf, C. (2016). *ADHD and Psychotherapy*. http://jonathanh averkampf.ie/wp/wp-content/uploads/2016/09/ADHD-and-Psychotherapy-1.pdf.

Heatherton, T., & Wagner, D. (2011). Cognitive neuroscience of self-regulation failure. *Trends In Cognitive Sciences*, *15*(3), 132-139. https://doi.org/10.1016/j.tics.2010.12.005

Hinshaw, S. (2010). *The Mark of Shame: Stigma of Mental Illness and an Agenda for Change: Stigma of Mental Illness and an Agenda for Change*. Oxford University Press.

Hirsch, O., Chavanon, M., & Christiansen, H. (2019). Emotional dysregulation subgroups in patients with adult Attention-Deficit/

Hyperactivity Disorder (ADHD): a cluster analytic approach. *Scientific Reports*, 9(1). https://doi.org/10.1038/s41598-019-42018-y

Hoogman, M., Bralten, J., Hibar, D., Mennes, M., Zwiers, M., & Schweren, L. et al. (2017). Subcortical brain volume differences in participants with attention deficit hyperactivity disorder in children and adults: a cross-sectional mega-analysis. *The Lancet Psychiatry*, 4(4), 310-319. https://doi.org/10.1016/s2215-0366(17)30049-4

Howell, C. (2020). *Frederick the Great - potato king*. The Lit & Phil. Retrieved 19 July 2021, from https://www.litandphil.org.uk/blog/posts/2020/june/frederick-the-great-potato-king/.

I Don't Need to Be Fixed! Epiphanies of Self-Acceptance from Adults with ADHD. ADDitude. (2020). Retrieved 28 July 2021, from https://www.additudemag.com/self-acceptance-adult-adhd/.

Instanes, J., Klungsøyr, K., Halmøy, A., Fasmer, O., & Haavik, J. (2016). Adult ADHD and Comorbid Somatic Disease: A Systematic Literature Review. *Journal Of Attention Disorders*, 22(3), 203-228. https://doi.org/10.1177/1087054716669589

Jackson, O. (2021). *Ascending Diverse Learners*. Presentation, NEIU Student Research and Creative Activities Symposium.

Kessler, R., Adler, L., Barkley, R., Biederman, J., Conners, C., & Demler, O. et al. (2006). The Prevalence and Correlates of Adult ADHD in the United States: Results From the National Comorbidity Survey Replication. *American Journal Of Psychiatry*, 163(4), 716-723. https://doi.org/10.1176/ajp.2006.163.4.716

Kinzer, N. *What It Looks Like To Accept Your ADHD — Nikki Kinzer • Take Control ADHD*. Nikki Kinzer • Take Control of your ADHD. Retrieved 28 July 2021, from https://takecontroladhd.com/blog/category/what-it-looks-like-to-accept-your-adhd.

Kolar, D., Keller, A., Golfinopoulos, M., Cumyn, L., Syer, C., & Hectman, L. (2008). Treatment of adults with attention-deficit/hyperactivity disorder. *Neuropsychiatric Disease And Treatment*, 4(2), 389-403. https://doi.org/10.2147/ndt.s6985

Kooij, J., Bijlenga, D., Salerno, L., Jaeschke, R., Bitter, I., & Balázs, J. et al. (2018). Updated European Consensus Statement on diagnosis and treatment of adult ADHD. *European Psychiatry*, 56(1), 14-34. https://doi.org/10.1016/j.eurpsy.2018.11.001

Kross, E., Bruehlman-Senecal, E., Park, J., Burson, A., Dougherty, A., & Shablack, H. et al. (2014). Self-talk as a regulatory mechanism: How you do it matters. *Journal Of Personality And Social Psychology*, 106(2), 304-324. https://doi.org/10.1037/a0035173

Kuja-Halkola, R., Lind Juto, K., Skoglund, C., Rück, C., Mataix-Cols, D., & Pérez-Vigil, A. et al. (2018). Do borderline personality disorder and attention-deficit/hyperactivity disorder co-aggregate in families? A population-based study of 2 million Swedes. *Molecular Psychiatry*, 26(1), 341-349. https://doi.org/10.1038/s41380-018-0248-5

Langberg, J., Dvorsky, M., & Evans, S. (2013). What Specific Facets of Executive Function are Associated with Academic Functioning in Youth with Attention-Deficit/Hyperactivity Disorder?. *Journal Of Abnormal Child Psychology*, 41(7), 1145-1159. https://doi.org/10.1007/s10802-013-9750-z

Larsson, H., Chang, Z., D'Onofrio, B., & Lichtenstein, P. (2013). The heritability of clinically diagnosed attention deficit hyperactivity disorder across the lifespan. *Psychological Medicine*, 44(10), 2223-2229. https://doi.org/10.1017/s0033291713002493

Lee, E. (2014). Adam Levine Stars in New PSA About His ADHD Struggle: "When I Can't Pay Attention, I Really Can't". *US Weekly*. Retrieved 28 July 2021, from.

Lewis, L. *Body Doubling: The ADHD Tool We Should All Be Using.* HealthyADHD | Info, Coaching, & Community for Women. Retrieved 30 July 2021, from https://healthyadhd.com/body-doubling-for-adhd/.

Lindblad, A., Ting, R., & Harris, K. (2018). Inhaled isopropyl alcohol for nausea and vomiting in the emergency department. *Canadian Family Physician Medecin De Famille Canadien, 64*(8), 580.

Linehan, M. (2015). *DBT skills training handouts and worksheets* (2nd ed.). The Guilford Press.

Litz, R. (2009). *The Mango: Botany, Production and Uses* (2nd ed., pp. 58-60). CABI.

Loeber, R., Burke, J., Lahey, B., Winters, A., & Zera, M. (2000). Oppositional Defiant and Conduct Disorder: A Review of the Past 10 Years, Part I. *Journal Of The American Academy Of Child & Adolescent Psychiatry, 39*(12), 1468-1484. https://doi.org/10.1097/00004583-200012000-00007

Matthews, M., Nigg, J., & Fair, D. (2014). Attention deficit hyperactivity disorder. *Current Topics In Behavioral Neurosciences, 16*, 235-266. Retrieved 26 July 2021, from.

McCarthy, S., Asherson, P., Coghill, D., Hollis, C., Murray, M., & Potts, L. et al. (2009). Attention-deficit hyperactivity disorder: treatment discontinuation in adolescents and young adults. *British Journal Of Psychiatry, 194*(3), 273-277. https://doi.org/10.1192/bjp.bp.107.045245

Miller, G. (1956). The magical number seven, plus or minus two: Some limits on our capacity for processing information. *Psychological Review, 63*(2), 81-97. https://doi.org/10.1037/h0043158

Mikami, A. (2010). The Importance of Friendship for Youth with Attention-Deficit/Hyperactivity Disorder. *Clinical Child And*

Family Psychology Review, 13(2), 181-198. https://doi.org/10.1007/s10567-010-0067-y

Morgan, P., Staff, J., Hillemeier, M., Farkas, G., & Maczuga, S. (2013). Racial and Ethnic Disparities in ADHD Diagnosis From Kindergarten to Eighth Grade. *PEDIATRICS, 132*(1), 85-93. https://doi.org/10.1542/peds.2012-2390

Mueller, A., Fuermaier, A., Koerts, J., & Tucha, L. (2012). Stigma in attention deficit hyperactivity disorder. *ADHD Attention Deficit And Hyperactivity Disorders, 4*(3), 101-114. https://doi.org/10.1007/s12402-012-0085-3

Naples, M. (1979). *Effective frequency*. Association of National Advertisers, Inc.

National Center for Health Statistics. (2015). *Association between diagnosed ADHD and selected characteristics among children aged 4–17 years: United States, 2011–2013. NCHS data brief, no 201.* Centers for Disease Control and Prevention.

National Center for Health Statistics. (2015). *National Health Statistics Reports Number 81: Diagnostic Experiences of Children With Attention-Deficit/Hyperactivity Disorder.* Centers for Disease Control and Prevention.

Oram, J., Geffen, G., Geffen, L., Kavanagh, D., & McGrath, J. (2005). Executive control of working memory in schizophrenia. *Psychiatry Research, 135*(2), 81-90. https://doi.org/10.1016/j.psychres.2005.03.002

Orlov, M. (2010). The ADHD Effect on Marriage. Specialty Press.

Otterman, D., Koopman-Verhoeff, M., White, T., Tiemeier, H., Bolhuis, K., & Jansen, P. (2019). Executive functioning and neurodevelopmental disorders in early childhood: a prospective population-based study.

Child And Adolescent Psychiatry And Mental Health, 13(1). https://doi.org/10.1186/s13034-019-0299-7

Ozcelik, H., & Barsade, S. (2011). WORK LONELINESS AND EMPLOYEE PERFORMANCE. *Academy Of Management Proceedings, 2011*(1), 1-6. https://doi.org/10.5465/ambpp.2011.65869714

Phelps, M., & Abrahamson, A. (2008). *No limits: The will to succeed.* Free Press.

Piferi, R., & Lawler, K. (2006). Social support and ambulatory blood pressure: An examination of both receiving and giving. International Journal Of Psychophysiology, 62(2), 328-336. https://doi.org/10.1016/j.ijpsycho.2006.06.002

Quinn, P., & Wigal, S. (2004). Perceptions of girls and ADHD: results from a national survey. *Medscape General Medicine, 6*(2), 2. Retrieved 27 July 2021, from.

Rau, S., Skapek, M., Tiplady, K., Seese, S., Burns, A., Armour, A., & Kenworthy, L. (2020). Identifying comorbid ADHD in autism: Attending to the inattentive presentation. *Research In Autism Spectrum Disorders, 69,* 101468. https://doi.org/10.1016/j.rasd.2019.101468

Reale, L., Bartoli, B., Cartabia, M., Zanetti, M., Costantino, M., & Canevini, M. et al. (2017). Comorbidity prevalence and treatment outcome in children and adolescents with ADHD. *European Child & Adolescent Psychiatry, 26*(12), 1443-1457. https://doi.org/10.1007/s00787-017-1005-z

Robinson, L., Thompson, J., Gallagher, P., Goswami, U., Young, A., Ferrier, I., & Moore, P. (2006). A meta-analysis of cognitive deficits in euthymic patients with bipolar disorder. *Journal Of Affective Disorders, 93*(1-3), 105-115. https://doi.org/10.1016/j.jad.2006.02.016

Santosh, P., Baird, G., Pityaratstian, N., Tavare, E., & Gringras, P. (2006). Impact of comorbid autism spectrum disorders on stimulant response in children with attention deficit hyperactivity disorder: a retrospective and prospective effectiveness study. *Child: Care, Health And Development, 32*(5), 575-583. https://doi. org/10.1111/j.1365-2214.2006.00631.x

Seneca, L. (054 AD). As quoted in N. Potter (2019), *The Meaning of Pain: A radical new approach to overcoming chronic pain.* Hachette UK.

Shiller, R. (2020). *Narrative Economics: How Stories Go Viral and Drive Major Economic Events.* Princeton University Press.

Schneider, J. (2007). Behavioral persistence deficit in Parkinson's disease patients. *European Journal Of Neurology, 14*(3), 300-304. https://doi.org/10.1111/j.1468-1331.2006.01647.x

Scott, W. (1962). Cognitive Complexity and Cognitive Flexibility. *Sociometry, 25*(4), 405. https://doi.org/10.2307/2785779

Siebner, H., Limmer, C., Peinemann, A., Drzezga, A., Bloem, B., Schwaiger, M., & Conrad, B. (2002). Long-Term Consequences of Switching Handedness: A Positron Emission Tomography Study on Handwriting in "Converted" Left-Handers. *The Journal Of Neuroscience, 22*(7), 2816-2825. https://doi.org/10.1523/ jneurosci.22-07-02816.2002

Silverstein, M., Faraone, S., Leon, T., Biederman, J., Spencer, T., & Adler, L. (2018). The Relationship Between Executive Function Deficits and DSM-5-Defined ADHD Symptoms. *Journal Of Attention Disorders, 24*(1), 41-51. https://doi.org/10.1177/1087054718804347

Singh, H., Meyer, A., & Thomas, E. (2014). The frequency of diagnostic errors in outpatient care: estimations from three large observational studies involving US adult populations. *BMJ Quality & Safety, 23*(9), 727-731. https://doi.org/10.1136/bmjqs-2013-002627

Sprafkin, J., Gadow, K., Weiss, M., Schneider, J., & Nolan, E. (2007). Psychiatric Comorbidity in ADHD Symptom Subtypes in Clinic and Community Adults. *Journal Of Attention Disorders, 11*(2), 114-124. https://doi.org/10.1177/1087054707299402

Stevens, F., Hurley, R., & Taber, K. (2011). Anterior Cingulate Cortex: Unique Role in Cognition and Emotion. *The Journal Of Neuropsychiatry And Clinical Neurosciences, 23*(2), 121-125. https://doi.org/10.1176/jnp.23.2.jnp121

The European market potential for mangoes. Cbi.eu. (2021). Retrieved 29 July 2021, from https://www.cbi.eu/market-information/fresh-fruit-vegetables/mangoes/market-potential.

Tierschutzverordnung (TSchV) 455.1 (2018). Geneva.

Trinko, J., Land, B., Solecki, W., Wickham, R., Tellez, L., & Maldonado-Aviles, J. et al. (2016). Vitamin D3: A Role in Dopamine Circuit Regulation, Diet-Induced Obesity, and Drug Consumption. *Eneuro, 3*(3), ENEURO.0122-15.2016. https://doi.org/10.1523/eneuro.0122-15.2016

Van der Kolk, B. (2014). *The Body Keeps the Score: Brain, Mind, and Body in the Healing of Trauma by Bessel van der Kolk.* Penguin Books.

Volkow, N., & Swanson, J. (2013). Adult Attention Deficit–Hyperactivity Disorder. *New England Journal Of Medicine, 369*(20), 1935-1944. https://doi.org/10.1056/nejmcp1212625

Volkow, N., Wang, G., Newcorn, J., Kollins, S., Wigal, T., & Telang, F. et al. (2010). Motivation deficit in ADHD is associated with dysfunction of the dopamine reward pathway. *Molecular Psychiatry, 16*(11), 1147-1154. https://doi.org/10.1038/mp.2010.97

Walitza, S., Drechsler, R., & Ball, J. (2012). Das Schulkind mit ADHS. *Therapeutische Umschau, 69*(8), 467-473. https://doi.org/10.1024/0040-5930/a000316

Weikard, M. (1775). *Der philosophische Arzt.* Der Andreaeischen Buchhandlung.

Why does Volkswagen make sausages? Reasons Behind the Currywurst. Elgin VW. (2020). Retrieved 29 July 2021, from https://www. elginvw.com/blog/why-does-vw-make-sausages/.

Wilens, T., Adamson, J., Monuteaux, M., Faraone, S., Schillinger, M., Westerberg, D., & Biederman, J. (2008). Effect of Prior Stimulant Treatment for Attention-Deficit/Hyperactivity Disorder on Subsequent Risk for Cigarette Smoking and Alcohol and Drug Use Disorders in Adolescents. *Archives Of Pediatrics & Adolescent Medicine, 162*(10), 916. https://doi.org/10.1001/archpedi.162.10.916

Wilens, T., & Spencer, T. (2010). Understanding Attention-Deficit/ Hyperactivity Disorder from Childhood to Adulthood. *Postgraduate Medicine, 122*(5), 97-109. https://doi.org/10.3810/pgm.2010.09.2206

Made in the USA
Coppell, TX
04 March 2024

29726773R00070